# FIELDS OF MAROON AND GOLD

A ramble through
Northamptonshire cricket
1974 to 2013

ANDY ROBERTS

Other books by the same author:

Thanks For The Wembleys (Northampton Town FC) – 2005

Flying The Flag: The UK In Eurovision - 2009

First published 2014 by AJR Publishing

Photographs by Pete Norton Photography Ltd

ISBN: 978-1490939728

# ABOUT THE AUTHOR

Andy Roberts was born in Northampton in 1962 and has followed the fortunes of the town's sporting teams since he can care to remember.

He worked at the Chronicle & Echo, then Northampton's evening newspaper, between 1984 and 2000 and was fortunate and privileged to cover both Northamptonshire County Cricket Club (1988 to 1994) and Northampton Town Football Club (1994 to 2000) for the newspaper.

He is married to Alison, who does not share his sporting obsession, with three boys Zach, Jake and Harry - who do!

# ACKNOWLEDGEMENTS

There are many people to thank for making this book possible and for allowing me to wallow in some wonderful childhood memories.

Not least David Capel, for providing the inspiration from years ago, and Steve Coverdale for providing a comprehensive overview of the years he was involved with the cricket club.

My sincere thanks also to Rob Bailey, Geoff Cook, Winston Davis, Nigel Felton, Andrew Hall, Dennis Lillee, David Ripley and David Steele for their kind contributions.

And to photographer Pete Norton, for once again turning up trumps with some fine photographs.

I would like to dedicate to this book to all 'absent friends' – players, officials, supporters, colleagues, writers - especially all those who made the cricket circuit such fun back in the 1980s and 1990s and who are, sadly, no longer with us.

In particular the late journalists Martin Searby (Yorkshire), Gerald Mortimer (Derbyshire) and the Telegraph's Dicky Rutnagur. Wonderful company, lovely memories!

# MILESTONES

# SIGNPOSTS

| | |
|---|---|
| 13 | COLIN MILBURN |
| 17 | MUSHTAQ MOHAMMAD |
| 18 | DAVID STEELE |
| 19 | BISHAN BEDI |
| 20 | SARFRAZ NAWAZ |
| 22 | PETER WILLEY |
| 29 | JIM WATTS |
| 30 | GEOFF COOK |
| 34 | WAYNE LARKINS |
| 40 | ALLAN LAMB |
| 42 | DAVID CAPEL |
| 45 | KAPIL DEV |
| 46 | ROB BAILEY |
| 47 | DAVID RIPLEY |
| 49 | WINSTON DAVIS |
| 52 | STEPHEN COVERDALE |
| 57 | ROGER HARPER |
| 73 | DENNIS LILLEE |
| 77 | ALAN FORDHAM |
| 95 | GREG THOMAS |
| 96 | NIGEL FELTON |
| 103 | CURTLY AMBROSE |
| 153 | MIKE PROCTER |
| 154 | PAUL TAYLOR |
| 155 | KEVIN CURRAN |
| 185 | ANIL KUMBLE |
| 198 | DAVID SALES |
| 202 | MAL LOYE |
| 203 | DEVON MALCOLM |
| 212 | MATTHEW HAYDEN |
| 216 | MICHAEL HUSSEY |
| 219 | KEPLER WESSELS |
| 221 | ANDRE NEL |
| 224 | GRAEME SWANN |
| 226 | MONTY PANESAR |
| 232 | CHRIS ROGERS |
| 233 | ANDREW HALL |
| 235 | LANCE KLUSENER |
| 248 | ALEX WAKELY |
| 250 | DAVID WILLEY |

# FIELDS OF MAROON AND GOLD

Northamptonshire, Middle England. A county that folk tend to pass through on their way to somewhere more exciting. And that is a shame.

Its history is one of strategic significance – it was once an important administrative centre, it backed the Parliamentarians against the Royalists during the English Civil War, with Charles I defeated in the decisive battle at Naseby, and it remains home to famous spires and squires.

Not least, it is here you also find the final resting place of the People's Princess, Diana Spencer, on the Althorp estate.

Its geography is good, unless you are fond of being beside the seaside.

In Northamptonshire you are as far away from the sea as you can possibly get.

But if you prefer the bright lights or a bit of culture, it is a handy base for London, Birmingham, Oxford, Cambridge and Stratford-upon-Avon, all just an hour away.

And its sporting base is excellent, boasting league football at Sixfields (though this might have changed as you read!), premiership rugby at Franklin's Gardens and horse racing at Towcester.

Not forgetting that the county is the motorsport capital of the world with racing on the oval at Rockingham, stock car racing at Brafield and banger racing at Santa Pod.

And, most significantly, Northamptonshire welcomes petrol heads from all over the globe every year to the Formula One British Grand Prix at Silverstone, the home of British motor racing.

But what is there to say about its cricket team and those proud to have worn the maroon and gold Tudor Rose?

Well, successful years have been very few and far between and there has certainly been little to shout about in recent times.

The Twenty20 Cup triumph at Edgbaston in 2013 came as something of a shock, representing as it did Northamptonshire cricket's first major trophy in a whopping 21 years.

The memories of Allan Lamb lifting the NatWest Trophy at Lord's in 1992, and before that Jim Watts the Benson & Hedges Cup in 1980, were very distant ones.

The cricket team has had its moments over the years but, in summary, it is a story of long and inglorious struggle, a story that is as enduring as it is endearing.

While this roundhead county has never really found favour in the courts of appeal, either in historical or cricketing terms, the maroon and gold has nevertheless served up a cavalcade of cavaliers up there with the very best.

My exciting liaison with Northamptonshire cricket began in the early 1970s, when the larger-than-life Colin Milburn and his flailing sword held sway in the kingdom.

The love affair burgeoned surveying the majesty of Wayne Larkins, Peter Willey and Allan Lamb in full glorious flight.

And the romance was recently re-kindled on a late summer's night in Birmingham in 2013, when a young pretender by the name of David Willey – son of Peter – wielded his flashing blade to put posh old Surrey in their place.

An outcome only bettered had the opposition been Middlesex, or maybe Kent.

The side may not have won a great deal but late chairman Lynn Wilson's credo was to 'keep attacking' and that commitment has marked Northamptonshire out as one of English cricket's most colourful and entertaining sides over the years.

From the moment I took my first tentative steps through the Wantage Road gates, on a murky day in late May 1973, this much was clearly apparent.

Wantage Road, as a venue for first-class cricket in the early 1970s, was bleak, ramshackle, monochrome and overwhelmingly uninspiring. But the field of play was ablaze with colour.

From the sartorial selection of Bishan Bedi's turbans of many colours to the vivid and beguiling stroke play of Mushtaq Mohammed, the stylish craftsmanship of Wayne Larkins – the very personification of a cavalier - and the obdurate character of the silver-haired roundhead David Steele, a bespectacled hard nut with the straightest of bats.

Sadly, the career of 'Ollie' Milburn largely passed me. I must have seen him in play during my early days watching Northamptonshire, following the accident which resulted in him losing an eye, but I do not remember him.

I surely would have remembered him had I see him play before the accident, showcasing that hallmark of quality that set him apart from the rest.

As much a *bon viveur* as a *bon joueur*, Milburn's legacy would be perpetuated by future generations at Northampton.

My first match at Wantage Road was the tourist fixture against New Zealand early in 1973 and the talking point of a rain-affected match centred on the Kiwi opener Glenn Turner, who was prolific in county cricket with Worcestershire.

Turner scored 111 in the first innings of the match and so passed 1,000 first-class runs before the end of May.

A landmark that meant that a Northamptonshire match got a mention in the oracles of the day and this didn't happen often, and still doesn't happen often if truth be told!

Northampton actually lies south of the M1's Watford Gap, referring to Watford village in Northamptonshire.

But it lies north of the Hertfordshire town of Watford and it was this criterion which traditionally defined the interest in Northamptonshire's cricketers from selectors who very rarely liked to stray away from their home comforts in London town.

In truth, Lord's and the Oval were understandably preferable venues than Wantage Road, which was a sight for sore eyes for the more discerning cricket lover.

You see there were three in a rather peculiar sporting marriage at Northampton's County Ground, which by decree of an arrangement managed by the Cockerill Trust had to accommodate association football and bowls as well as cricket.

Up to October 1994, a three-sided football ground, home to Northampton Town Football Club (commonly referred to as the Cobblers), apologetically clung on to the northern face of the cricket outfield.

Moving west, from the Hotel End football terrace you would pass the cricket ground's tiny West Stand, home to the oldest and grumpiest cricket followers on the circuit.

On past the postage stamp-sized club shop, the scorers' old signal box and a plastic makeshift second scoreboard before arriving at the mound of 'green seats' which arced up to not a very great height.

On the south side came the ladies' pavilion, the hulking enclosure – with great views of the ground from the top to this very day – and the old pavilion, then home to the players and officials.

And looking east, to complete the circuit, there was little apart from the main scoreboard, a smattering of higgledy-piggledy seating, the ground staff's base and a view of the bowls club over the wall before you would reach the football ground's far from imposing Spion Kop terrace and its lowly main stand.

There was little to commend the ground but during the lazy, hazy summer days of school holidays in the 1970s, there was nowhere else this this impressionable young teenager would rather have been.

My first junior membership was taken out in 1974 and to this day I still have my folded blue membership card, containing all the fixtures, and a black leather autograph book full of signatures, many of them hard-fought.      **10**

Happy schoolboy memories remain of cricket games on the outfield during the intervals, splinters from the 'green seats' – my favourite vantage point on the ground – and packed lunches while watching the game while sat on one of the crowd control boxes plonked on the Hotel End.

Of getting backies to the ground on a mate's bike for a 20-minute ride to the ground, once it had been established that someone like Wayne Larkins, Peter Willey or Mushtaq Mohammed had come in to bat.

Of getting a pal into the ground for free, courtesy of a two-card shuffle which hoodwinked the unsuspecting gatemen – take two people in on two tickets at one end of the ground, exit at the other with two tickets and bring said pal in on the spare.

Of packets of hard gums from the corner shop, of proudly manning the rickety unofficial plastic scoreboard where the numbers kept falling off, of keeping meticulous scorecards in the John Player League matchday programme!

Of watching my hero Turner back in county action for Worcestershire and my namesake – the Antiguan head spinner Andy Roberts, the formidable West Indies fast bowler – battering the Northamptonshire batsmen as part of champion county Hampshire's attack.

The summer of 1975 was dominated by and belonged to a man of Steele, called up to England duty by Tony Greig to stick it up the touring Australians, in particular those terrible twin quickies Jeff Thomson and Dennis Lillee.

And, to an extent, it was also a hugely significant year for a young lad called David Capel who – at the tender age of 12 – was already making his mark on the local cricket scene with his home village side Roade.

But as far as a place in the Northamptonshire's first team?

Never in his wildest dreams did Capel imagine that within six years he would be sharing the same dressing room as his England hero.

## MAN OF STEELE

And never in his wildest dreams, close to retirement at the age of 33, did Staffordshire's David Steele expect a call to arms from the England team hierarchy in 1975.

The England team were in trouble and looked to Northamptonshire's 'man of Steele' to dig in against the old enemy.

And so, on Test debut at Lord's, with towels for thigh pads, Steele strode out into the middle dubbed by the press as 'the banker who went to war'.

But only after negotiating a little local difficulty, miscalculating the route to the middle and striding purposefully through a door which led to a basement toilet rather than the famous Long Room at headquarters.

And not withstanding a little playful banter from Thomson who greeted Steele's arrival with 'who have we got here, Groucho Marx?', or words to that effect.

No matter, the glasses were fixed, the cap was on, the gum was being vigorously chewed and the lips were all of a mutter. 'Stainless' Steele was ready to get stuck in to the Aussies.

Steele said: "It was a big surprise to be selected for England but to be honest I'd been pretty good form over a number of seasons. In one of them I was beaten to the 1,000 runs by Essex's Keith Fletcher, by around 20 minutes.

"1975 was a great year for me. I scored 1,500 runs that summer and it was also my Benefit Year.

"My mind was right and the distraction of the Benefit certainly helped me.

"I was going around the local pubs with pontoon boxes and I always had a collection of bats with me which had been signed by all of the Northamptonshire players.

"I remember the bats very well as they had written on them 'Pakistan genuine willow' and must have weighed all of a whopping 3lbs!

BURNOPFIELD, County Durham, England
COLIN MILBURN
Born: 23 October 1941
Death: 28 February 1990
Northamptonshire: 1960 to 1969/1973 to 1974
Nickname: Ollie
RHB/RM

"I told the lads 'whatever you do don't play with them' but there was no telling some people and needless to say there were soon a few shattered bats lying around!

"Ollie Milburn got a little bit precious and at one stage refused to sign a 3lb bat but I eventually persuaded him to do so!

"I admired Ollie and the way he was able to hit the ball, the eye for a shot, the technique.

"And I could understand why he would look down on 3lb bats!

"I remember him hitting 100 before lunch in a match at Nottingham and I thought to myself that this isn't the way it's meant to be!

"When Ollie was batting at Northampton, legend had it that the shops shut up because they knew folk would go up to the ground and see him in action.

"When he was out and I came in, the shops would open up again because everyone would go back into town!

"But I'd got a reputation for getting stuck in and not giving away my wicket lightly and I think that's why England came calling.

"The Australians were in their pomp and had some seriously-talented fast bowlers in Thomson and Lillee.

"Thomson's action was a thing of beauty, with his 'bow and arrow' shape at the point of delivery and he and Lillee were a formidable partnership. **13**

"Tony Greig called me up because he knew he needed a battler and a grafter in there against these two in particular.

"If you played for Middlesex or Kent in those days you had a much better chance of being recognised and selected for England than if you played for say Northamptonshire, Leicestershire and Derbyshire, the so-called unfashionable counties.

"But this wasn't a series for a fancy-dan from Middlesex or Kent so they called on a fighter from Staffordshire, playing for Northamptonshire.

"I loved the battle and the banter but I was determined that they would find it very hard to get me out.

"I was still prepared to have a go with my favourite hook shot. I got runs with it, I got out with it and I figured that if you lived by the sword you would have to accept you would also die by the sword.

"But the key for me was concentration. I chewed my gum and spoke to myself as the bowlers ran up, 'watch the ball, watch the ball'."

Steele's Test scores that summer were 50, 45, 73, 92, 39 and 66 – that success, built on defiance and character, won him the Sports Personality of the Year title at the end of the year.

He added: "What a year, 1975 definitely belonged to me; a Benefit, a Test debut and Sports Personality of the Year. What a fantastic memory and proof that sometimes dreams can become reality.

"I used to relish playing fast bowling. It wouldn't be true to say I enjoyed it, no-one enjoys playing the quicks and they'd be lying if they said they did.

"But for me it was a battle, a war of attrition. Front foot forward and bat behind, marvellous!

"Some could play the quicks better than others and here Allan Lamb is a clear case in point.

His record against the West Indians during the 1980s speaks for itself. **14**

"But you had to want to go out there and get stuck in. Some didn't want to and if you were one of those the quick bowlers would be able to smell you a mile off."

Steele had the winter to chew over a good deal with a local butcher, who presented him with a chop for every run he scored in his Benefit Year – that will be 1,756 chops, thanking you – and Steele's heroics earned him a place in the England side to face the West Indies the following year.

He scored a Test highest score of 106 against the Windies at Trent Bridge but, in spite of averaging 42 runs with the bat and less than 20 with the ball in an eight-match international career, he wasn't taken to India for the winter tour on account that he could not play slow bowling.

Steele said: "The knock at Trent Bridge was the highlight of my career. It was an unforgettable day, even if I was out hooking!

"Another innings that sticks out for me was a match against Somerset early in my career when the opposition thought I was on drugs because I was batting like Milburn!

"Early in the game we lost three wickets for just one run and I found myself batting with Roger Prideaux, facing Fred Rumsey who bowled left-arm over.

"The field was up and Fred was on fire. When he hit you the ball seemed to go through the pad and it bloody hurt.

"I got through the pain barrier on adrenalin and somehow began to get some shots away.

"I don't know why or how, everything just seemed to click into place. The scoreboard read 30-3 and I'd scored 27 of them. It was unheard of and no-one could quite believe it.

"In the end I managed 64 out of a score of 76 and Roy Virgin congratulated me on an 'incredible innings'. That's one I'll always remember!"

Steele remained philosophical after his Test rejection and took some comfort in the fact that the late Jim (EW) Swanton, the doyen of cricket writers and commentators, would now have no trouble recognising him.

**15**

Steele said: "When I met Jim Swanton for the first time, I must admit I had very little time for him. He came across to speak to me and my cousin Brian Crump and said to us 'now which one's Steele and which one's Crump?'

"I ask you! I mean, Brian had started off at 5ft 8ins and had shrunk to 5ft 6ins on account of bowling 10,000 overs.

"And here was this guy sitting in Fleet Street with no idea who my cousin was, probably because he couldn't get beyond watching Middlesex and Kent. He asked where I was from. I told him I was from Stoke-on-Trent, had he heard of it?

"On one occasion at Lord's, he came over to me and said 'for a front foot player I was surprised, you actually played off your back foot quite a bit'. To which I replied 'I have got two feet and am able to use both!'

"Over the years we got to know each other and in time I became quite fond of him. One season he was at the Parks in Oxford at the start of the season and we walked to the pavilion together.

"He said: 'England is a wonderful place from May to September, then it's bye'. I remember asking him what he meant by 'bye'?

"'Bahamas' came the reply. 'And you?' Er, Stoke?! I don't think it quite sunk in how anyone could possibly spend the winter in England.

"Journalist Alex Bannister did make me chuckle when he told me that Swanton was the biggest snob he had ever come across.

"Alex said that Swanton would have a chauffeur to ferry him around but he would still travel in the other car! That tickled me!"

The long hot summer of 1976 produced runs aplenty across the country, Willey and Roy Virgin putting on a record county fourth-wicket stand of 370 against Somerset at Northampton.

Virgin, who opened, amassed 145 against his former club and Willey hit a career-best 227.

JUNAGADH, Gujarat, India
MUSHTAQ MOHAMMAD
Born: 22 November 1943
Northamptonshire: 1966 to 1977
RHB/LB

Steele recalled: "I remember Will sharing this massive stand and scoring a fine double century but at the end of the day he sat in the dressing room, sorted out his poorly knee and then disappeared off home.

"There was no stopping behind for a little celebration. That was Will, he didn't like fuss or standing on ceremony."

Steele and Willey shared the dressing room for many seasons and delighted in winding each other up.

They respected each other as cricketers but didn't always see eye to eye, Steele often commenting upon Willey's gruff demeanour by declaring that 'happiness was Will shaped!'

Steele said: "Peter was a tremendous cricketer and I had a huge amount of respect for him but we always liked to get under each other's skin.

"He never wasted words and it was difficult to get a smile out of him.

"Put it this way, I wouldn't have wanted to go on holiday with him. But my wife Carole thought differently and she loved him to bits!

"As a cricketer though cometh the hour then cometh the man. He was the ideal man for you when the chips were down.

"He played for England and adopted a Barrington stance at the crease which opened him up and gave him more freedom to play.

"He was a very versatile player but was hampered by a knee injury. At first he would bowl quick seamers but later reverted to off-spinners.

**17**

BRADELEY, Staffordshire, England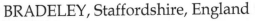
DAVID STEELE
Born: 29 September 1941
Northamptonshire: 1963 to 1978/1982 to 1984
Nickname: Crime
RHB/SLA

*David Steele signing autographs at Wantage Road
– still a sports personality after all these years!*

---

"He was the sort of player who as a teenager looked much older than he was and he had the strongest forearms in the business. I mean, even Ian Botham didn't dare mix it with Will!"

Willey held firm with the bat at Lord's to help Northamptonshire to their first-ever domestic honour – the 1976 Gillette Cup.

 AMRITSAR, Punjab, India
BISHAN BEDI
Born: 25 September 1946
Northamptonshire: 1972 to 1977
RHB/SLA

*Bishan Bedi pictured together with Australian batsman Mike Hussey – both served county cricket in Northamptonshire with distinction*

---

## END OF THE DROUGHT

One-day kings Lancashire, boasting a fearsome line-up, were uprooted as soon as Farokh Engineer's stump was sent cartwheeling out of the ground by a delivery from left-arm paceman 'Doctor' John Dye.

Although David Hughes breathed life into the Red Rose innings late on with 26 off an over from Bedi, their total was never enough.

 LAHORE, Pakistan
SARFRAZ NAWAZ
Born: 1 December 1948
Northamptonshire: 1969 to 1982
RHB/RFM

Virgin and Willey got the Northamptonshire reply off to a fine start, putting on 103 for the opening wicket, and man-of-the-match Willey saw the Tudor Rose home by six wickets.

Mushtaq became the first county captain to hoist aloft some silverware and, having finished second in the Championship behind Middlesex, Northamptonshire cricket was riding the crest of a wave.

Big things were expected in 1977 but sadly they didn't materialise – what did materialise was the spectre of Australian business tycoon Kerry Packer casting a large shadow over domestic cricket.

County secretary Ken Turner's response after a disappointing season was to clear out the old guard, a controversial move which shook the club's foundations to the core.

Steele said: "Ken Turner was very old school tie and swept away a lot of talented cricketers. Bob Cottam had gone the year before and then we lost Mushtaq, Bedi, Dye and Virgin.

"I think this was a bad move on Ken's part. We had won the Gillette Cup in 1976, and come close to winning the Championship, I think if we'd have kept a lot of the players who were released then we would still have had a title chance the following year.

"Mushtaq was a super all-round cricketer who never got the praise he should have done. He was a gem from an early age, I think he scored a century for the Pakistani Eaglets in Peterborough when he was only 15 or 16.          **20**

"I found myself paired up with Mushtaq quite a few times and as three and four we carried the batting along with Geoff Cook and Peter Willey.

"Bishan was a delight to observe. He was always in total control, physically and mentally. You cannot coach the mentality of a successful spin bowler. You either have it or you don't and Bishan clearly had it.

"Many just haven't got the mentality that you need out there. There's a great Yorkshire saying that 'it's no use knocking on the door if there is no-one inside.' There was never a truer word spoken!

"Bob Cottam had also gone and the heart of our bowling attack had just been ripped out. Bob was a class bowler who had joined us from Hampshire but at one point in his time at Northampton he suffered dreadfully from the yips.

"In a match at Old Trafford in 1975 he was bowling with the new ball and just couldn't control it. It got to him and things came to a head in a Sunday League game when he went for 70 runs off his eight overs.

"Somehow John Dye got the blame and the two of them ended up having a fight in the pavilion, with skipper Jim Watts quite happy to let them get on with it!

"In one game at Northampton, we were still in the old pavilion and Bob was getting changed in the toilets. Bishan Bedi came into the dressing room and said 'have you heard Bob, he's talking to his boots?'

"Sure enough, we found Bob kneeling down in the toilets with seven pairs of boots laid out in front of him and he was asking the boots 'which of you lot is going to bowl straight for me today?'

"The yips can be a dreadful thing and they have affected so many players over the years.

"I went to Derbyshire for a number of seasons and there they affected a player called Fred Swarbrook. He totally lost it, he was a left-arm spinner and just couldn't get the ball to pitch where it needed to.

**21**

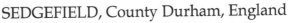SEDGEFIELD, County Durham, England
PETER WILLEY
Born: 6 December 1949
Northamptonshire: 1966 to 1983
RHB/OB

*Peter Willey trying out David Steele's specs for size – a dressing room double act which kept the rest of the troops entertained!*

-----------------------------------------------------------------------------

"In one game against Lancashire we were up against it and Peter Kirsten suggested that Fred might as well have a bowl, saying 'he's having the sack in August, he may as well enjoy it'.

"By this stage, Fred had taken to carrying a lucky pebble around with him, convinced it would help his bowling. The pebble was in his pocket, and he would give it a rub before he ran up to bowl.

"Well the first ball was a full toss which the batsman misjudged, the second bounced twice down the track and again the batsman messed up. **22**

"I thought bloody hell, how have they not scored any runs off this shit?!

"Then Bernard Reidy, aiming a sweep, pulls a muscle and has to retire hurt!

"And who should the next batsman be but Clive Lloyd?! At which point Fred was advised to bowl the pebble instead of the ball! Needless to say, Fred stuck with ball and Lloyd sent it out of the ground by a good distance!"


## THE BOY FROM ROADE

David Capel was making observers sit up and take notice, scoring runs in his teens and clearly establishing himself as a young batsman of immense promise.

A brief dalliance with neighbouring village side Stoke Bruerne left a lasting impression on Bruerne stalwart Graham Alsop, who had embarked on a commercial role with Northamptonshire alongside enterprising secretary Turner.

Alsop said: "For too many years I played alongside David's father John in a Stoke Bruerne team that won almost every trophy it competed for.

"John would bring along his two boys David and Andrew, himself no slouch with the bat, to the cup finals we played in.

"On one occasion John asked if it would be possible for me to take David to a Benson & Hedges Cup game at the County Ground.

"In those days, complimentary tickets were few and far between at a club forever counting its coppers, so Plan B came into operation.

"John delivered David to my house and he climbed into the back of a Commer van which was, at that time, the only vehicle the club owned.

"We arrived at gates and were waved through - some things never change do they?!

"I let David out onto the ground and he later assured me that it was then that he decided his future would be as a county cricketer, and possibly an international cricketer too.

"As he went on to accomplish both, how pleased am I that he made that journey in the back of the van!"

Capel said: "At that time, Graham Alsop had just started working part time on the commercial side at the club.

"I knew him from Stoke Bruerne and he also had strong links with Pianoforte in Roade.

"I wanted to see that match at the County Ground because Kent were the visitors and I wanted to watch Bob Woolmer – he had just scored a Test century and was the player of the moment."

The stepping stone trail from schools cricket and then village cricket in the Town League led to the more glamorous County League with Horton House, where Capel cut his teeth enjoying both the game and the social scene that went with it.

When Horton matched up against the Northampton Saints cricket side, two of the county's best young cricketing prospects found themselves in opposition.

In the Saints ranks was a young lad of similar age, Duncan Wild, who had attended Northampton School for Boys.

This was also my alma mater and I found myself in the same school year as Wild.

And I can still vividly remember Wild running through our form cricket team, dismissing us for next to nothing with the highest scorer being Mr Extras!

Capel said: "As a 15-year-old I played for the county U19s, together with Duncan who was the other local boy making good.

"Duncan scored a century for the Saints aged 13 and was extremely-highly rated.

"He could definitely play and was a very accomplished batsman and a fine fielder. We were always pushing each other to be top dog."

**24**

Capel's love for cricket, and Northamptonshire cricket in particular, shone through in the way he approached and played the game.

And it was Brian Reynolds, revered as a guiding father figure to many youngsters who made it onto the books at Wantage Road, who offered him the opportunity to transfer to headquarters and play for the County Colts.

The quantum leap to the pinnacle of the county game with Northamptonshire was almost complete.

Capel said: "I had spent long hours in the nets at the County Ground where I got noticed by those at the club on the lookout for promising youngsters.

"Brian Reynolds was also scouting around the nets, at the time Brian was the Second XI captain and coach! Brian was the main man for me, he was the dad at the club – he had the discipline of a sergeant major, a stern but benevolent figure.

"I'll never forget the day when the sweaters in Northamptonshire colours were presented. I was totally made up – I laid them out on a chair in my room and stared at them, hardly daring to believe that they were mine!

"During the winter, I worked for the shoe manufacturer Kettering Surgical Appliances, making cricket boots for Derek Underwood, Mike Hendrick and Graham Dilley and earning £50 a week!"

Capel enjoyed a good first year in the Colts fold, under the tutelage of Roy Wills and former England U19 captain Bob Carter, who both made him feel part of the set up.

Joining Northamptonshire around the same time as Capel and Wild was a tall and powerful batsman from Steele's backyard of Staffordshire, Rob Bailey.

Going out of the door though was Steele, one of Bailey's boyhood heroes, who was switching to Derbyshire for 1979 – a path that Bailey would follow years later at the end of his Northamptonshire career.

The astute Bailey recognised at an early stage the fierce intensity that would characterise Capel the cricketer.  **25**

Bailey said: "We had both joined the Northamptonshire staff as young lads and I think it is fair to say that there were more talented all-rounders at the club than Capes at that particular time.

"But Capes had a great will and desire to succeed and he worked very hard to make sure he became the best all-rounder at the club. He did this through sheer determination.

"He joined just before me but naturally enough we were often paired up and I got to spend a lot of time away from home with him, in particular in South Africa.

"We have always been good colleagues and friends but we are very different.

"Capes has always lived and breathed his cricket. I have always liked to switch off at the end of a working day, but Capes would talk cricket whenever and wherever.

"I can recall an amusing moment early on in our time at Northamptonshire although I think at the time I probably didn't see the funny side.

"We were rooming together, I think in Manchester, and had both got an early night.

"I remember waking up to see Capes standing at the end of my bed, dressed smartly in blazer and tie, saying he was going down for breakfast and what would I like ordering?

"Something didn't seem quite right, not least because outside it was still pitch black.

"I looked at the time and saw it was 3am and asked him why he wanted to go to breakfast at this particular time?!

"Capes checked his own watch, which had stopped at six o'clock and he was that focused on getting up and ready for a day's cricket that he hadn't realised it was a little earlier than he thought!"

Batting remained Capel's main focus in second-team cricket but he also wanted to prove himself with the ball.

Capel said: "I scored 92 in an early game for the stiffs at Old Trafford and the reports went that I had 'the makings of a good opening bat.

**26**

"I broke my finger in a match against Glamorgan but began to realise that I could bowl as well as bat. I was competitive and wanted to do it all.

"Bowling opportunities were limited as we had the likes of Chris Booden, David Eland, Les McFarlane, Bob Carter and the returning Alan Hodgson all in the frame."

Geoff Cook – the Northamptonshire opener and vice-captain under Jim Watts – remembers the young new recruits arriving at Wantage Road at the turn of the decade.

Cook said: "Brian Reynolds was scouting around for promising young cricketers in the area and David was one of the fellows who benefited.

"He was identified as a local talent and introduced to the club as part of an organised campaign to increase Northamptonshire representation in the county side.

"David arrived alongside Duncan Wild, who also displayed a lot of talent, and Rob Bailey who had been spotted in Staffordshire cricket.

"In the past, Northamptonshire had relied on an investment of players from elsewhere in the country, counties like Durham, Staffordshire and Bedfordshire.

"But the management were keen to promote young talent to complement the likes of myself, Wayne Larkins, Peter Willey and Robin Boyd-Moss."

Capel looked up to the likes of skipper Jim Watts, the future captain Cook, boyhood influences Willey and Larkins and a certain young South African who had been blazing a trail since arriving in England the year before – Allan Lamb.

Capel said: "Cookie made me feel I wasn't just some bit part 16-year-old. He made me feel valued and developed a good team spirit.

"Lamby was a class act and I always had the utmost respect for him as a cricketer.

"Ned Larkins is best remembered as an opening batsman but when he first joined Northamptonshire he would bat down the order, normally at five.

"Ned would often say that Mushtaq Mohammad showed a lot of faith in him and gave him the confidence that he desperately needed.

"Ned disliked waiting around to bat. When he was switched to opener there was no time to wait around and this suited him so much better.

"With a top five batting line-up of Cook, Larkins, Williams, Lamb and Willey, opposition teams were reluctant to set us targets.

"And we didn't have the bowling attack to force matches from that perspective and with pitches not conducive to getting results we struggled to make an impact in the three-day game."

On the one-day front it was a different matter, with Northamptonshire again reaching the Gillette Cup Final in 1979, although on this occasion they were comfortably beaten by Somerset.

A year later they returned to Lord's for a Benson & Hedges Cup final date with Essex.

Capel said: "Lamby scored a good 72 to get us into a good position and word came down to the Tavern, from twelfth man Bob Carter via the secretary, that us youngsters could go up to the dressing room.

"I recall that there was a clear expectation that we would win and it seemed that this belief was instilled by the captain Jim Watts.

"Sarfraz and Jim Griffiths did the business with the ball. Sarfraz was a serious player having taken nine wickets in a game against Australia earlier that year."

In 1981, Watts stood down from the captaincy and Cook stepped up to the plate. Cook said: "It was an awkward time for the club. The likes of Bishan Bedi and Mushtaq had been let go four years previously and Sarfraz was now coming to the end of his career.

"We were at the end of the Kerry Packer era and there was plenty going on which had to be managed.                       **28**

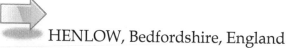 HENLOW, Bedfordshire, England
JIM WATTS
Born: 16 June 1940
Northamptonshire: 1959 to 1980
LHB/RM

"The squad I had wasn't really that strong, we had some good batsmen but struggled in the bowling department and, to this day, Northamptonshire has always had to balance its personnel against tight finances.

"However when the late Lynn Wilson was at the helm, the club was able to invest in some quality signings and towards the end of the decade good bowlers like Winston Davis, Curtly Ambrose and Greg Thomas came in.

"I think Northamptonshire has always punched above its weight in county cricket because the county really does not boast that many players or clubs.

"In my home county of Durham, like in Lancashire and Yorkshire, club cricket produces a great volume of young players which the county club is able to tap into."

Capel's first-class debut came in July against the touring fledgling Sri Lankans, just a few days before a certain Ian Botham put the Australians to the sword in THAT Test at Headingley.

"I only got a call up the night before because someone had pulled out of the team. Both Pete Mills and I were given a chance on a belting pitch in front of a decent County Ground crowd.

"The warmth of both the weather and the crowd made for a great feelgood occasion. Nothing ever changed after that, the Northampton crowd was always good to me.

The club highlight in 1981 was the 60-over campaign and the side reached the final of the inaugural NatWest Trophy, meeting Derbyshire at Lord's. **29**

MIDDLESBROUGH, Yorkshire, England
GEOFF COOK
Born: 9 October 1951
Northamptonshire: 1971 to 1990
RHB/SLA

Memorable staging posts along the way were the demolition of the Somerset of Botham, in his England pomp, and Viv Richards at Northampton and then a tense quarter-final rain-affected victory over rivals Leicestershire at a steamy Grace Road in the quarter-finals where Willey held sway.

A titanic semi-final against one-day giants Lancashire at Wantage Road arguably remains the greatest and most tense spectacle the old ground has ever witnessed.

To cut to the chase, in fading light late on a dull August evening, Northamptonshire's last pair Tim Lamb and Jim Griffiths somehow held out for 13 overs against the fearsome West Indies paceman Michael Holding, nicknamed 'Whispering Death' and then the world's fastest bowler.

Number ten bat Lamb held his nerve at the death, asking the umpires what was required for victory as darkness descended and doing his utmost to protect 'rabbit' number eleven Griffiths at the other end.

The pair prevailed for a one-wicket victory and Griffiths was chaired off the field by a band of ecstatic spectators, one of them being yours truly!

The 1981 NatWest competition was memorable as both semi-finals went right to the wire and the final itself was decided in Derbyshire's favour on account of the Peakites having lost fewer wickets with the scores tied.

Capel recalled: "Geoff Cook scored a very good century in the final which won him a place on tour to India although he was gutted to lose what was a very tight match. **30**

"I was pleased for him. What I always admired about Geoff was his very enterprising captaincy and that he would always set challenging declarations in the longer game.

"We had limited resources but we were always bold in our play, we played without fear. You could do that more in the 1980s as there were no promotion or relegation issues to distract you.

"The ethos was always to attack the opposition, win or lose it was definitely a case of keeping on attacking".

Steele recalled the final well, it was to be his last game for Derbyshire and he went out on a high, not least because a return to Northampton beckoned.

He had enjoyed three years with the Peakites but found driving to Derbyshire from his Northamptonshire home tiring and he was pleased to be given the opportunity to return to Wantage Road to finish his first-class career where it had all started.

Steele said: "My final game for Derbyshire was the NatWest Trophy final against Northamptonshire in 1981, which we won off the last ball.

"It was a cruel way to win a match and a Cup final at that. I sought out the Northamptonshire secretary Ken Turner after the game and I said to him 'hard luck sec'. After a little bit more conversation I asked him 'can I come back?'

"My back was stiff as a board from all the travelling, to and from Derby for the home games alone.

"Ken shook my hand and said he'd get it sorted, saying 'we might have lost a match but at least I've got you back for next season'.

"My role on my return was as a senior player, to help some of the younger cricketers coming through and to play more as an all-rounder down the order.

"So I left the club in 1978, batting at three, and returned to the club in 1982 as a number seven bat and a slow left-armer required to bolster a bowling attack which wasn't very strong.

"I was relishing the chance to turn my arm over, as in my first spell I never got that many opportunities with Bishan Bedi in his pomp.

"Bishan could bowl teams out on dry pitches but when we played with uncovered pitches, and the pitch was wet, I would usually get among the wickets."

"But the side was still being re-built in 1982 and with Sarfraz now also out of the picture, our pace attack was very thin.

"Neil Mallender was learning the ropes, Jim Griffiths and Tim Lamb were our main seamers, and they basically wound me up and stuck me on at one end.

"We had some promising young batsmen who were developing in Rob Bailey, David Capel, Robin Boyd-Moss and Duncan Wild.

"Ken had said he wanted the team built around me and the batting was not a problem, in fact the top five picked themselves - Geoff Cook, Wayne Larkins, Peter Willey, Allan Lamb and Richard Williams, a terrific line-up."

Steele's return co-incided with Capel getting more chances in the first team, batting at seven in the three-day game and bowling a little.

Bailey was also being afforded more senior opportunities and so, together with Capel, found himself sharing the dressing room with a cricketer both had admired in their younger years.

Bailey said: "When I was a young lad in Staffordshire, David Steele came to a presentation evening at my school and it was some event.

"At the time, he was the Sports Personality of the Year so it was a tremendous honour having him visit us.

"I was sitting in the hall and all of a sudden David started waving in my direction.

"It was only then that I realised he was waving at my dad who was sitting next to me, the two of them having played cricket together for Staffordshire. **32**

"One of the highlights of my career was playing in the same cricket team as David Steele. At the bar after a game he would always have half a shandy and of course you knew you would be paying!

"David prized his wicket in any form of cricket, no matter what the competition. I can remember a NatWest Trophy game at Swindon against Wiltshire in 1983 when he batted the last seven overs for a five not out when we were looking to get more runs on the board!

"Peter Willey went spare but in the end we won the match comfortably. A not out was very important to David!"

Capel said: "Steele and Willey had been my Northamptonshire heroes in my early teens, Willey had been my first autograph! Playing with both of them a few years later was a dream come true.

"I will always remember some wise words from Steeley after getting a second innings duck, thanks to a non-turner from the late Chris Balderstone on my Championship debut.

"We'd both scored nought in that match and his philosophy that he shared with me was 'any man can smile when life goes along like a song, show me a man who can smile when things go wrong!' And one of my other favourite Steeley sayings was 'show me the person and I'll tell you about the cricketer!'"

## FORGET ME NOT OUTS AND RUN OUTS

David Steele acknowledged the importance of walking off the field with a 'not out' star against your name and said: "I liked collecting 'not outs'. Some would say that made me a selfish batsman but I didn't see it that way at all.

"Coming in at seven, as I did in my second spell with Northamptonshire, I was getting the dregs of the innings. I felt I deserved a not out and that I was within my rights to go out and get a star by my score.

ROXTON, Bedfordshire, England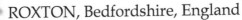
WAYNE LARKINS
Born: 22 November 1953
Northamptonshire: 1972 to 1991
Nickname: Ned
RHB/RM

*Wayne Larkins – making the headlines*
*with some stunning innings in the early 1980s*

"Wayne Larkins went ballistic in a match against Glamorgan at Swansea and at lunch we had nearly 200 on the board. That was inconceivable in those days.

"We notched up a huge score and, batting low down the order, I got ten. I said to myself that I didn't want to be doing that again!

"So I started on my quest for the not out, for the star. Often in matches when you had the joke bowlers on late doors you could help yourself to a decent score and a star to boot.

"In one match at Old Trafford I scored 30 and 25, both not out scores. I was over the moon!

"Headlines were being written about 'the man they can't get out' and I began to develop a little bit of an obsession with it.

"I started thinking about setting records for not out scores and wondering what the world record for not out scores was! It got to a point when I began dwelling on it on the field and at home and it really tensed me up."

And Steele's return to Northamptonshire renewed friendly fire 'hostilities' with Willey, who before too long would also be seeking out pastures new.

Steele said: "I remember coming into the dressing room at Northampton on my first day back.

"Peter Willey would always be the first one in, followed by yours truly. As I was hauling my coffin into the dressing room, Will turned to me and said 'what are we doing signing you up again you old bugger?'

"I thought that's a nice welcome and replied 'well Will, I am back and I don't come cheap. I've signed a very good contract, and part of my contract is that I sit next to you in the changing room.'

"Will wasn't happy with that and I repeated 'it's in the contract!'

"Quick as a flash, he whisked along to the secretary's office to check out what was what!"

The Steele and Willey show kept the younger players in the dressing room entertained.

Willey's forearms were the stuff of legend but Steele would often like to test the strength of the aforementioned limbs.

Especially on one occasion when he made light of a Willey dismissal and found himself hung up on a clothes hook by his sweater!

He would often test the patience of his team-mates and on another occasion he batted so slowly in a Sunday League match that he was not allowed back into the dressing room and had to change back at home!

Also given the nickname 'Crime' (as in crime doesn't pay), a nod to the fact that he liked to cadge drinks as well as fags from his fellow players, Steele also made a packet of chewing gum go a long way.

Steele said: "I used to like chewing gum when I was batting.

"It helped me concentrate but there was only one problem. I didn't care much for the spearmint flavour.

"So when the mint was chewed out, I liked the gum without flavour and at the end of the day would stick the chewed gum on my peg in the dressing room.

"But I got a lot of stick from my team-mates for leaving my gum all over the place.

"There was almost an incident at the card table on one occasion when John Dye went to leave the table only to find his trousers stuck to the bottom of the table by one of my used pieces of gum.

"I had to laugh on returning to the dressing room at the start of one season because the painters had been in to give the dressing room a bit of a facelift and had painted over the bits of gum I'd left on my peg.

"So everyone knew which had been my peg. But it wasn't ideal because I had to go out and buy some fresh gum!"

Steele relished the senior player role and was tasked with a number of duties for away games. He said: "For many of the away games I was the driver and my little Red Mini was packed to the rafters.

"I'd invariably have Alan Hodgson, all six foot whatever, hunched in the front seat. And there would be Cookie and Ned smoking fags to the dozen in the back.

"We'd have some great fun on those drives, sometimes not getting to our hotel until the early hours of the morning because my passengers wanted a drinks break!

"On one trip I remember we stopped off at an orchard in the middle of nowhere because Ned fancied throwing a few apples around.

"Then we went looking for a pub and as we finally drove around the country lanes looking for our hotel the car appeared to be awash with apples, they were everywhere, on the floor, on the seats, rolling along the top of the dashboard!

"I was also designated to transport the team's first aid black box and I also took along a push ha'penny board. They were good days!"

Steele, while now coveting his not outs, was still an expert in the field of 'run outs' – much to the chagrin of many partners at the crease.

This was encapsulated perfectly by one cameo at the County Ground when the hapless Richard Williams was left stranded by Steele, who nonchalantly leaned on his bat having kept his ground while his partner huffily strode back to the pavilion. Not for the first time...

Steele said: "I was quite well known for running people out during my career. I was very good at it. The one that sticks with me was the time we beat the touring Australians at the County Ground in 1972.

"We'd got a narrow first innings lead and then Bishan Bedi, who took nine wickets in the match, did the business again with the ball in the second innings.

"We needed 120-odd to beat the Aussies and I was opening the batting in the second innings.

"Geoff Cook and Mushtaq got out and we needed 20 runs to win when my cousin Brian Crump came to join me at the wicket.

"I remember the ball going to the boundary by the West Stand, the place where those who don't understand cricket used to sit.

"I called for a second run because I spotted the fielder was the Aussie opener Bruce Francis, not a great fielder in general.

"On this occasion though he picked up the ball and returned it over the top of the stumps like a bullet.

"Brian, his head well back, was run out by a good three yards and trudged back to the pavilion, out for one.

"I thought to myself 'I'll be hearing from him later'. But it wasn't a bad day – I'd got 60 runs, a star by my name and we won the match!"

While at Derbyshire, Steele famously ran out Geoff Miller and later told his colleague 'oh well Geoff, that's show business'.

Some while later, Steele was on the receiving end of a poor run out call and made his way back to the dressing room, only to be greeted by all of his team-mates singing and dancing 'that's show business!' It's a story he dines out on!

Steele could be as bloody minded as another stubborn individual plying his trade for Yorkshire, Geoffrey Boycott.

He had played in the game against Yorkshire at Northampton in his first spell where John Hampshire staged a 'go slow' in protest against Boycott's single-minded run-making.

Steele said: "I couldn't believe it. Bill Athey had scored a ton and then Yorkshire needed to get from 285 to 300 in plenty of time to pick up a fourth batting point and they didn't get there. It was pathetic!                                                 **38**

"Boycott was in the habit of getting changed at home and driving to the club in his whites. I don't know what that was all about and I couldn't be doing with that.

"But what a player he was, such a focused individual. I loved the story of him and the Aussies and his habit of blocking the ball into the ground.

"Their bowlers would shout 'Hey, Fiery, flick us the ball'. Would he? Would he heck as like! He'd just stare down the track and tell the bowler 'come and fetch it!'

"And then there was Viv Richards, what a player! He could play shots that no-one else could! He always had a bit of a feud with Bob Willis and one shot I will always remember is of Viv picking up a Willis delivery which went over mid-off for six. It was magnificent!

"But then we also had a couple of excellent, gifted stroke players at Northampton at the time. Ned Larkins was a wonderful player to watch, and he was at his best during my second spell with the club.

"He was always so positive. Ken Turner, although he'd never played the game professionally, certainly knew how to spot a cricketer.

"I remember in one match the opposition being very pleased at having removed the considerable threat that was Larkins.

"It was one of Allan Lamb's early first-team games in 1978 and I remember Geoff Cook telling the opposition wicketkeeper 'wait until you see the next man in, he's something else'.

"Allan had it all as a batsman. He was very relaxed off the field, and liked to mess around, but once he had a bat in his hand he was completely in the zone. It was the rate that he scored his runs which set him apart from those around him."

Steele held strong views, and still does, about the politics that habitually got in the way of nurturing young talent at Northamptonshire. **39**

LANGEBAANWEG, South Africa
ALLAN LAMB
Born: 20 June 1954
Northamptonshire: 1978 to 1995
Nickname: Lamby
RHB/RM

*Allan Lamb – his style never wavered, Lamby kept on attacking as a player and captain for Northamptonshire and as a fearless batsman for England who stood up to the might of the West Indies*

**40**

He said: "The Cricket Association used to do a lot of good work developing young cricketers in the county.

"But the county club never ever developed a worthwhile relationship with the NCA and for me this was a crying shame.

"David Capel came up through the NCA ranks, as did my boys Mark and Aaron, and so too the Swann brothers Graeme and Alec and the likes of Duncan Wild and Kevin Innes.

"But there always appeared to be a real stand-off between the club and the NCA and this was as much driven by the egos of the men in charge, respectively Ken Turner and John Malfait.

"Both were good men but it was their way or the highway and this attitude didn't really change when Steve Coverdale replaced Ken Turner.

"John Malfait was very well liked and his good work laid the foundations for what later became the cricket club's academy.

"The club had to look to nurture and develop young talent, having relied for many decades on recruiting from minor county heartlands such as Durham and my own Staffordshire.

"But at the end of my career it was good to see young players like Rob Bailey and David Capel coming through into first-team reckoning.

"I remember being at the crease when David scored his first Championship century but he really only got into the side as a seam bowling option and he went on to develop into a top-class all-rounder, added to that he was a good athlete in the field.

"David would often say that bowling was really hard work and he was bloody right, it was, especially if you were a fast bowler.

"Frank Tyson and John Snow, both brilliant fast bowlers, would testify to that." **41**

NORTHAMPTON, England
DAVID CAPEL
Born: 6 February 1963
Northamptonshire: 1981 to 2012
RHB/RFM

*David Capel – a homespun lad
demonstrating the style that won
him many admirers at Wantage
Road, and beyond*

# ON THE LASH!

The Championship match against Yorkshire at Middlesbrough held great significance for the emerging Capel.

He said: "Geoff and Ned smashed the ball everywhere against a side containing the likes of Geoffrey Boycott, Chris Old, Graham Stevenson and Phil Carrick.

"Near lunch on the second day I got a bowl. Boycott was there looking for a hundred which, in his mind's eye I think, he'd already got inked in.

"I was bowling military medium pace with a bit of inswing but decided to run the fingers over the seam and go for a leg cutter, a variation ball.

"The ball held up a little, Boycott played for midwicket and got a leading edge and Neil Mallender took the catch at mid-off.

"Boycott out and Cook's master plan comes off as he'd put me on just a couple of overs before lunch in the hope of a breakthrough!

Steeley, with an unsmiling face, came over and said to me 'two overs and you've got him, I've been trying to do that for 20 years!'"

Boycott became Capel's first Championship wicket, a fact not lost on the Yorkshire and England legend.

Boycott said: "David informed me that I gave him his first Championship wicket. I had a little joke with him, saying that I couldn't remember the dismissal and that I didn't lose any sleep over it!

"I mean, I was knocking on a bit at the time at the age of 41. I was as good as past it! In truth I did remember it, caught by Neil Mallender bowled David Capel for nine runs.

"I've always liked David as an honest, straightforward cricketer and was pleased to offer him advice and encouragement during his career. And I am glad I made a young man's day!"

Capel would go on to enjoy the regular tussles with Yorkshire.

A county that quite literally would become very close to his heart as it was in Scarborough that he was to meet his future wife Debbie.

And he developed a good friendship on and off the field with Larkins and Williams, the three of them would regularly be found together in the bar chewing the cud after a day's play.

Capel said: "I admired the sporting philosophy and attitude of Wayne Larkins.

I loved the way he played the game, he had inherited a lot of the soul that rubbed off from the way characters like Colin Milburn and Mushtaq Mohammad went about their business.

"On his day he was peerless, a majestic right-handed strokemaker who could take attacks apart at will."

Larkins had a reputation for playing hard on and off the field.

He enjoyed a drink, a fag and a bet to help him relax after a day's cricket.

Capel added: "He enjoyed the social side of the game after a day's play and would talk about all manner of things including cricket.

"This would help put him in the right frame of mind for the following day's play. It wouldn't work for everyone but for Ned it did."

At the end of the season a disillusioned Peter Willey, unhappy at the terms offered him by Northamptonshire, upped sticks for Leicestershire.

His exit opened up the team selection frame, with the side going through further transition.

Steele missed the banter with his old sparring partner but recalled one of his favourite Will moments involving a young hopeful at the club.                    **44**

 CHANDIGARH, Punjab, India

KAPIL DEV
Born: 6 January 1959
Northamptonshire: 1981 to 1983
RHB/RFM

Steele said: "Will always said exactly what he thought and I remember once when a young lad from Bedford called Ian Peck sought him out for some advice on his batting.

"Will was in the nets with Peck who asked him if he could spare a little time to give some advice around his technique.

"As he always did, Will sat down with the bat between his legs and watched Peck in the nets and the exchange at the end of the net went something like this:-

Peck: 'What do you think?'
Will: 'I know your trouble.'
Peck: 'Yes?'
Will: 'You can't play.'
Peck: 'Thank you.'"

"That was typical Will, say it how it is. Ian Peck took it well and we always have a little chuckle about it when we meet!

"The best match I had with Will was in a big win against Sussex at Eastbourne. Kapil Dev was in our side, he was a wonderful striker of a cricket ball but he didn't really want to bowl.

"We put on a big score on a benign pitch but all of a sudden it began to turn square. Will and I bowled unchanged to win the match, with Kapil taking a number of fine catches close to the bat.

"Some do the business, some fall away. I wasn't one to fall away and neither was Will, it was a job well done.    **45**

BIDDULPH, Staffordshire, England
ROB BAILEY
Born: 28 October 1963
Northamptonshire: 1982 to 1999
Nickname: Bailers
RHB/OB

*Rob Bailey – one of the nicest guys in*
*cricket, respected player and umpire*

 LEEDS, Yorkshire, England
DAVID RIPLEY
Born: 13 September 1966
Northamptonshire: 1984 to present
Nickname: Rips
RHB/WK

*David Ripley – jumping for joy following a successful career as player and coach, guiding Northamptonshire to Twenty20 glory in 2013*

"I think there is a bright future beckoning for his son David. If he has his father's heart, desire and attitude, and from what I've seen so far he has, he will go a long way."

Capel's maiden century came, after injury, against Somerset in 1983 – coming to the wicket at 135-5, he scored an unbeaten 109 out of a score of 336-9 declared.

Bailey said of his colleague: "Capes saw himself as a very capable batsman and indeed he was. He thought he could bat at four, but I never saw his as a number four batsman.

"He was always a five or a six. Batting in the first four is a completely different ball game to batting anywhere else in the order.

"His strength was as a middle-order batsman with the capability of leading the attack as a fast bowler."

Bailey and Capel found themselves in the thick of it when the 'young lions' were pitched into the Northamptonshire side to face the touring West Indians at Manor Fields, Bletchley in 1984.

Also in the line-up was a young wicketkeeper from Leeds, David Ripley, who had been snapped up from under Yorkshire's noses as cover for first-choice George Sharp, who nearing the end of his career.

Ripley said: "My first game was against Leicestershire at Grace Road and I was also selected to play in the tour match that year.

"When George retired in 1985, Stuart Waterton came in from Kent and I was up against him for the gloves for a couple of years."

And in the West Indies party at Bletchley was fast bowler Winston Davis, who was later to join Northamptonshire in 1987.

Now living in Bewdley, Worcestershire, Davis is a tetraplegic having been left severely paralysed following a fall while cutting out branches from a tree in his native St Vincent in 1998.

**48**

KINGSTOWN, Saint Vincent, West Indies
WINSTON DAVIS
Born: 18 September 1958
Northamptonshire: 1987 to 1990
Nickname: Winnie
RHB/RF

*Wayne Larkins and Winston Davis – Winnie has kept in touch with many of his old mates since his accident in 1998*

-----------------------------------------------------------------

Davis remembers the whole 1984 experience fondly, admitting that the scene in England was a bit of an eye-opener. He said: "I was fortunate to be part of that incredible West Indies squad that summer.

"I got called into the squad as a replacement for Ezra Moseley and played in the Test at Old Trafford.      **49**

I managed to score 77 as night-watchman and shared in a double century stand with Gordon Greenidge.

"At this time, the West Indies had four outstanding fast bowlers in Andy Roberts, Malcolm Marshall, Michael Holding and Joel Garner so it was difficult to get a look in as a bowler.

"Any side with four quality fast bowlers will win matches at any level and so it proved for the West Indies in the 1980s.

"There are some outstanding cricketers around now but not too many bowlers. The advent of Twenty20 cricket has created quite a few star batsmen but it is not a form of cricket that suits the bowler!"

At the end of the 1984 season, Steele retired from county cricket, shortly before his 43rd birthday.

Much preferring to wear a cap at all times he did however once try to experiment, unsuccessfully, with wearing a helmet.

Steele said: "I was one of the old school who didn't care much for wearing a helmet when they were introduced.

"I wore a helmet just once, facing up to West Indian fast bowler Sylvester Clarke who was lethal and the most feared quickie in county cricket.

"He was a deceptive bowler and I decided to go for the helmet. Well, you've never seen anything like it!

"It was like trying to put a helmet on a lighthouse, the thing wouldn't sit properly and the glasses got in the way as you can imagine!

"Seeing what was going on, Sylvester came over to me and said 'Steeley, don't lower yourself'. I replied 'what are you going to do then Sylvester, bowl me a few spinners are you?!

"Anyway, I couldn't be doing with that thing on my head and he helped me take the helmet off and it was taken down to the boundary edge.

"The first ball after all that carry one whizzed past my ears and I gave him a look as he came up to me. **50**

"All he said was 'back in business!' And he was absolutely right, we were back in business. I loved that!"

Secretary Ken Turner also stepped down from secretarial duties during the winter and handed over to Steve Coverdale, a former Cambridge Blue who had spent several years at Yorkshire playing second fiddle to wicketkeeper David Bairstow.

Coverdale came in as secretary/manager in 1985 and recalled an 'early warning' around Capel's potential to develop into a top-class cricketer.

He said: "I couldn't remember Capes at all from my playing days although I suspect we would have played against each other in Second XI cricket at Horton in 1982.

"I kept wicket for Yorkshire in that game and scored a century.

"Rob Bailey was certainly playing for Northamptonshire because he has claimed for more than 30 years that I cheated him out in that match!

"The captain Geoff Cook had marked my card, saying that he thought Capes was potentially a very fine cricketer but was too intense.

"Geoff felt that the intensity needed to be reined back and he was very keen to get him bowling as well as batting.

And Peter Willey, who had moved to Leicestershire although I believe his heart always remained in Northamptonshire cricket, echoed Geoff's views.

"He too told me he felt David was too intense and needed to relax a lot more and actually work less to become a better cricketer.

"What always struck me was David's work ethic – it was tremendously intense, almost phobic you could say.

"He would practise, train, and constantly seek advice from coaches. Cricket was at the heart of everything and obsessional wouldn't be too strong a description and it was almost as if he thought he would make himself ill if he wasn't working and practising.                                                    **51**

 YORK, Yorkshire, England
STEPHEN COVERDALE
Born: 20 November 1954
Northamptonshire: 1985 to 2003
RHB/WK

*Stephen Coverdale – the club's
long-serving secretary/manager and chief
executive who drove the modernisation
programme at Wantage Road alongside
chairman Lynn Wilson*

"This intensity characterised him but perhaps also handicapped him. He put a lot of pressure on himself to achieve and, as a consequence, I think in the early days both the successes and failures were magnified.

"David saw himself as a batsman and didn't seem too keen to get himself bowling. He wasn't totally reluctant but clearly felt that it got in the way of his enjoyment of batting.

"He failed to appreciate what a good bowler he was potentially. It didn't click for a while but the penny finally dropped that the bowling was his passport to play at a higher level.

Geoff Cook added: "David's emergence as a quality all-round cricketer, was just what Northamptonshire needed, a very capable batsman and bowler in the shape of one player!

"David was absolutely right to develop his all-round skills and it served him very well. By the end of his career he had become a terrific wicket-taking bowler, displaying a huge amount of skill and no shortage of pace.

"His athleticism was not in question, when injuries did not intervene, and he had a nice sprinkling of aggression in his armoury.

"As a cricketer, David was a little bit ahead of his time – the overt ambition, not being afraid to suffer fools and the ability to recognize the need to address the physical side of his training programme to ensure he conditioned himself before and during the season. He recognised the need to do it.

"He was a match-winning cricketer and often his sheer drive took him to the edge. He was very ambitious and so driven that at times he would behave a little bit selfishly.

"He developed new bowling skills and was able to score runs very quickly with the bat, which all made him a very valuable team member, albeit one you often had to reason with and run with at the same time.

"I found that he was sometimes ahead of the rest of team in his match thinking and he was a very positive lad to have around.

**53**

"He was a decent catcher of the ball and would like to field at slip to conserve his energy, laudably learning from the likes of Clive Rice and Richard Hadlee."

Around this time, Capel was inevitably already being spoken of as the heir apparent to Ian Botham but Coverdale believed the pressure put on the player by the media in this respect was totally unfair.

He said: "David was constantly being judged against Botham, whose exploits for England had been legendary.

"A lot of young all-rounders at that time came under a very harsh media and public spotlight but David probably more than anyone. All it did was build further pressure on him which really was the last thing he needed. David always felt he could have made it into the England team purely as a batsman but I never thought that to be the case.

"If he'd stayed just with his batting I think he would have developed into a high-class county player but I don't think he would have played for England.

"He would have been fighting for a place in the era of Mike Gatting, David Gower and Allan Lamb and I fear he would have been part of that overlooked generation, suffering a similar fate to the likes of Rob Bailey and Neil Fairbrother who got limited opportunities."

Coverdale believes that Capel would have found it easier to cope in the modern day game on the back of the greater support mechanisms which are now available for professional cricketers to tap into.

He said: "The now common usage of sports science and psychology provides cricketers with both physical and mental support, which just wasn't around 20-25 years ago.

"It would certainly have benefited me – as a player at Yorkshire under Ray Illingworth, talk of psychology was interpreted as a sign of ineptitude and weakness.

"As my career progressed I would tend to dwell and worry about doing something wrong rather than doing something well. **54**

"When I played for Yorkshire, mention was always made of that fine Yorkshire wicketkeeper Jimmy Binks and that he would never allow himself to drop more than one ball a session, even if that was a wild throw from the boundary.

"It was made clear that was the standard expected. So say if I failed to gather a bad throw during the first half hour of a session that would be on my mind - the fear of failing would always be with me.

"Nowadays, it is about accentuating the positive – Sir Alex Ferguson, as Manchester United manager, would always talk about 'what we need to do'.

"Ferguson is a great role model for sports management, in as much that as a 70-year-old man he was able to relate to 17-year-old youngsters on the staff at Old Trafford.

"One thing I quickly realised is that the approach and attitude of young cricketers was very different to what had been the case twenty, ten or even five years earlier.

"They are now more materialistic and even selfish – wanting everything now - and the fact that Ferguson could cut through that and successfully integrate youngsters into a winning team was one of his great strengths."

Coverdale felt that Capel went on to powerfully assert his physical abilities and mental strength during the late 1980s.

He said: "David did require a lot of cajoling to develop as an all-rounder and he had to learn the skills and adapt his approach to the game pretty much on the hoof.

"He would often say that he could bat number three for any side in the country. I didn't think that he could but there was no denying his clear belief in his own abilities.

"He came to the club at roughly the same time as Robin Boyd-Moss, Rob Bailey and Duncan Wild.

"I remember Boyd-Moss being given a fast 'sporty' sponsored car by his sponsors, Wards of Wellingborough, and a lot of the other players at the time felt that they should be similarly blessed.

"One or two got really 'hung up' on the issue which frankly was nothing to do with the club and they were rather jealous!

"A few got distracted by non-cricketing issues and didn't progress as they certainly could have done, Boyd-Moss and Wild among them I suspect.

"Boyd-Moss returned to Kenya, Wild went into early retirement to pursue business interests.

"Bailey and Capel developed well and for Capes the likes of Wayne Larkins, Richard Williams and Roger Harper were all strong influences on him during that time."

Capel recalled a Harper innings in 1985 – a stunning 127 against Kent at Maidstone's Mote Park ground.

"I remember that he batted at seven in the match and I think it was Eldine Baptiste who bowled him a delivery that was a good length but probably straighter than it should have been.

"It wasn't a bad ball by any means but Roger hit this enormous six which was still rising as it left the ground.

"It was our first shot in anger, what Roger referred to as an 'ice-breaker' shot – bat hard but if you see you an opportunity to hit one then really nail it. You could see a collective shudder go through the Kent team and that one shot seemingly knocked the bowlers off their line and length.

"Roger was tremendous for us. A Guyanan, he was schooled in the Clive Lloyd way in his approach to cricket.

"We enjoyed each other's company on and off the field and he enjoyed some quiet time after a day's play, a little like Curtly Ambrose in later years.

"I played against Roger when we were both 19-year-olds – he was a 6ft 4ins spinner and in 40-over games he would have most of the fielders on the leg side and just a couple on the off side and he was happy to do the rest of the fielding on the off side off his own bowling!

"He was a tremendous athlete and a fielding inspiration, in fact our performance in the field was transformed. **56**

 GEORGETOWN, Guyana, West Indies
ROGER HARPER
Born: 17 March 1963
Northamptonshire: 1985 to 1987
RHB/OB

"I mean who can forget Roger's Test run out of Graham Gooch?! It was tremendous to have the world's best fielder in our team at the time."

Coverdale felt that Northampton had treated Capel well and that he would remain a 'home town boy' forever more.

He said: "His devotion to Northamptonshire cricket has been exemplary. Northampton has been very good for him, he earned the support of a large number of people in and around the club.

"He has family and ties in the county. Even when he had the chance to maybe go elsewhere later in his career, he remained loyal to his roots and even if the opportunity came along now for him to move away and pursue a cricketing career, I doubt he would do so.

"It works for some, but not for others. Jeremy Snape for example probably wasn't going anywhere at Northamptonshire, but he tried his luck elsewhere and ended up as a county captain and playing for England.

"But for others the grass most certainly doesn't turn out to be greener. There were a couple who moved from Northamptonshire in the belief that they were bettering themselves who came to me later – when things hadn't worked out as expected with their new clubs – and told me they had made big mistakes."

And in his first year in the County Ground hot seat, Coverdale also recalled his return to Headingley in the Sunday League – for a variety of reasons and one that went beyond the cricket! **57**

He said: "Yorkshire and Northamptonshire were both going great guns and we beat them in front of the television cameras off the last ball in what was our penultimate game, with Capes hitting a boundary.

"That took us to the top of the table with a real chance to win the league. Personally that meant a great deal but it also showed that a young team could hold its nerve to win tight matches.

"Unfortunately we lost our final game against Worcestershire and ended up outside the top three.

"But another reason that particular game sticks in the memory is because of a call I took early on the Sunday morning in the Queen's Hotel. It was Wayne Larkins on the other end of the line and I asked him where he was.

"He said he was in 'The Cells'. I enquired as to where that particular night club was, only for him to clarify that he was actually in the police cells after getting himself into a spot of bother!

"Ned didn't get much sleep that night but was back with us in time for the game, getting us into a winning position with a brilliant half-century and picking up a couple of wickets for good measure after we'd put Yorkshire in to bat."

In 1986, Northamptonshire bolstered their slow-bowling department with the astute signing of slow left-armer Nick Cook from neighbours Leicestershire.

And Capel fondly recalled a Championship game against Sussex that year, later to be dubbed – well at Wantage Road anyway – as the new Battle of Hastings.

Capel said: "We had been outplayed on days one and two and were set 300 or so to win on the final afternoon, on a very difficult pitch which deteriorated as the game progressed.

"Geoff Cook had broken his jaw so I opened the batting with Wayne Larkins, who was nursing a broken finger.

"Imran Khan was bowling well with the new ball in the second innings and it wasn't a pleasant experience.    **58**

"Robin Boyd-Moss was clean bowled for a duck, some deliveries were whizzing past the batter's nose and others were not getting off the deck.

"Before being bowled, Robin was almost killed by a flying ball off a length, a real neck ball which almost took his head off.

"I somehow managed to score a half century and later Allan Lamb took on the chase with Rob Bailey.

"The bounce of the pitch was unpredictable and the Sussex attack, apart from Imran, also included Colin Wells, Dermot Reeve and Tony Pigott.

"Lamby's brilliance got us home. It was superb and he completely knocked the bowlers off their line and length.

"He scored 157 on instinct as much as anything else. This amounted to roughly half the side's runs and we won by one wicket."

And the Championship game with Yorkshire at Scarborough at the end of the season proved another eventful affair.

David Ripley notched his maiden century against his home county, scoring an unbeaten 134 out of 422 to save the game.

But the youngster's achievement rankled with the Scarborough diehards, who wanted Northamptonshire to declare to enable Geoffrey Boycott to play his final innings for Yorkshire.

In the end, his first innings run out for 61 was the last stand in Yorkshire for one of England's most obdurate batsmen.

On to 1987, and a landmark pre-season for Capel who with Bailey represented England in a tournament in Sharjah.

In so doing, Capel became only the second Northampton-born player to represent his country, the only other being George Thompson back in 1910.

It was the first of 23 one-day internationals Capel would play - and all of them would be played overseas!  **59**

To put that remarkable statistic into context, from a pure box office perspective, a fit Botham would always be preferred by the selectors for a home series.

Capel and Bailey nudged the selectors with batsmanship of the highest quality in the Championship against Yorkshire at Northampton.

A game of sporting declarations set up a Northamptonshire victory target of 283 in 160 minutes plus 20 overs against the White Rose.

What followed saw the 'young lions' label firmly pinned on both Capel and Bailey's sweaters.

Having lost Geoff Cook and Larkins cheaply, and with Lamb also out and just 75 on the board, Capel joined Bailey in the middle with 208 still required - and not long to get them.

The pair of them put the Yorkshire bowlers to the sword, reducing the fielders to hapless bystanders.

Those were the days when many would leave their workplaces for the County Ground if a close finish was in prospect.

And accordingly there was a sizeable crowd in the ground at the death to cheer Northamptonshire home to an improbable and thrilling victory.

Capel paid tribute to Bailey that afternoon. He said: "Rob contributed an innings of the highest calibre in scoring an unbeaten 152.

"I thought to myself what a great player he was, he was brutal on that attack."

Northamptonshire won with nine balls to spare, Bailey and Capel's unbroken fourth-wicket partnership put together in fewer than 28 overs.

Bailey remembered the swelling number of spectators arriving at the ground in the hope of a good finish.

He said: "Word clearly got round quickly and Capes and I just went for it. Everything just went for us and Capes played brilliantly.

"It was a great run chase and it was always good to beat Yorkshire. We were both mobbed at the end and nearly got carried off the field!"

The match came a couple of days prior to Capel's Test debut, at the beginning of July, against Pakistan at Headingley.

He was picked as a swing bowler at Headingley but took no wickets – however he top scored for England with 52 out of 131 all out against a tricky Pakistani attack.

At county level, following the departures of Jim Griffiths and Neil Mallender, Capel now found himself leading the attack with Davis, who was sharing the overseas duties with Harper.

Capel said: "The pace attack was decent. There was Alan Walker, Duncan Wild and Gareth Smith in support and Nick Cook and Chippy Williams were our spinners.

"The bowling department held up pretty well but faded towards the end of the season.

"We got ourselves in a good position in the Championship but Nottinghamshire eventually went on to lift the title.

"At this stage of my career I was learning such a lot from the likes of Ned and Lamby, drawing on their ethos and style."

While it proved a case of 'so near but yet so far' in the three-day game, it was in the Cup competitions where the 'nearly men' tag stuck with a vengeance.

Northamptonshire set up a Final date in the Benson & Hedges Cup with a tremendous semi-final victory against Kent at Canterbury.

Capel said: "This was quite a match and we bowled first, Kent reaching 275 off their 55 overs.

"We thought it was gettable but Eldine Baptiste bowled very well with the new ball before a hamstring injury, taking figures of 1-8 from six overs in the match. **61**

"We lost a couple of early wickets in the reply and then another just before the tea interval and were well behind the run rate.

"I acted as Lamby's foil and he took them on, knocking the ball to all parts and finishing unbeaten on 126 in a five-wicket victory. That match saw him at his best."

Coverdale reflected on a tremendous victory, but one which wasn't without its drama at the very death.

He said: "Allan Lamb's innings was one of the great one-day innings of all time. Frankly when he went in we had little chance of winning the game.

"I was watching the game from the dressing room and it was a joy to see him seizing control and getting us back in with a chance.

"Cricketers are superstitious and I remember that as we were doing so well we didn't allow anyone to move from the seats they were sat in, just in case that brought us bad luck which would result in us losing a wicket.

"That meant that our captain, Geoff Cook, didn't see anything because he had sat down in a seat with no view to the ground!

"Lamby was ably assisted by Duncan Wild, Lamb doing the hitting and Wild putting in some hard running between the wickets.

"When Lamb thought he had hit the winning run, he walked off and there were tremendous celebrations in the dressing room. It was mayhem.

"But I knew that we hadn't won and that the scores were actually level. I think I was the only one who realised what the situation really was.

"So I literally had to grab hold of Lamby and told him 'We haven't won this, get it together - you've got to go back out and whatever you do don't get out!'.

"With the scores level we would win the game by virtue of losing fewer wickets.

"They did go back out. Lamby had a big slog from the next ball, got a thin inside edge past leg stump and we had won the game with two balls to spare but it was a little too close for comfort!"

## DOUBLE WHAMMY!

Yorkshire lay in wait at Lord's, a mere 11 days after they had been put to the sword by the 'young lions' in the Championship.

Capel said: "I had just played my first Test match and was in better nick with the bat than the ball. They won the toss and we were on the back foot on a very hot day.

"Richard Williams and I put on an important partnership to rebuild the innings and Chippy's experience shone through as the architect of the partnership."

In a tight match, the scores ended level and – as against Derbyshire in 1981 – Northamptonshire lost a showpiece game by dint of having lost more wickets than their opponents.

It was a day of mixed emotions for Coverdale, speaking up for Northamptonshire against his native Yorkshire.

He said: "It had been a bit of a breakthrough year for Capes who had come into his own as a bowler.

"But it was with the bat that he shone in the final at Lord's, making a fine 97 off the Yorkshire attack.

"He didn't open the bowling as he would usually have done, on the account that he felt he needed a bit of a breather after batting deep into our innings. I remember he talked Geoff Cook into that.

"That was probably a mistake for he had accounted for both Martyn Moxon and Ashley Metcalfe, the Yorkshire openers, in the Championship match just ten days before the final.

63

"I know they were worried about him. Winston Davis and Alan Walker opened up, Walker was initially expensive as Yorkshire got off to a flier and so too was Davis when he came back at the end.

"In between, Capes went for 66 runs off his 11 overs and we lost in spite of the scores being tied.

"Jim Love was named man of the match for his innings and this was very much a case of mixed feelings for me.

"We'd lost the match but Jim was a big mate, we'd grown up together at Yorkshire, and he was my closest friend in cricket. When we finally met some time after the game he gave me a big hug and I congratulated him although the defeat was hard to take.

"Especially, as the scorers confirmed, we only batted 54.5 overs. For some reason, Ken Palmer had let through a five-ball over.

"I don't know whether the extra ball would have made any difference but Palmer wasn't in the habit of doing us any favours!

"Ray Illingworth said to me a few days later that a Yorkshire win was 'the right result for cricket'. That was also hard to take."

More one-day agony was to follow in the NatWest Trophy, but spirits were high following a victory over the old enemy Leicestershire at Grace Road in the semi-final.

The county won with ease as Capel took out the top three in the Foxes order, including old boy Peter Willey - Williams's off-spin yielded him figures of 4-10.

That game led into a vital Championship game against title rivals Nottinghamshire at Trent Bridge.

For that reason, the team weren't allowed the opportunity to celebrate their semi-final victory – a decision which Coverdale, in hindsight, admits was a mistake.

He said: "We had won at Leicester on the Thursday afternoon with the big game against Nottinghamshire waiting for us on the Saturday.

"It was a top v second game and I decreed there would be no post-semi celebration on Thursday night, to allow for proper preparation for the weekend game.

"This was a big mistake. In hindsight, the players should have been allowed to let their hair down.

"On the Saturday, the pitch at Trent Bridge was like crazy paving and it was quite clear that whoever won the toss would win the match.

"Geoff Cook lost the toss and he didn't need to tell us the outcome. The look on his face said it all.

"We were a young inexperienced side on the whole and yet we were in the running for all the major prizes.

"However we only had a small squad and I think we ended up playing 28 out of the 31 days in August that year. Frankly the players were mentally and physically exhausted.

"As I said, the players should have been allowed to celebrate getting to the NatWest Final. They had earned that right. It was my mistake."

Nottinghamshire again loomed large for the NatWest Trophy final, a tough prospect.

In a match reduced to 50 overs because of poor weather on the Saturday, Northamptonshire posted a respectable 228-3, in the main thanks to 87 from Larkins and, in reply, Nottinghamshire slumped to 57-4 going into the reserve day on the Monday.

Naturally enough, spirits were high throughout Sunday going into the resumption although, ominously, Clive Rice was at the crease and Richard Hadlee was waiting in the wings.

Capel said: "It's still difficult to think about that second day. We dropped catches and also missed a run out in the Nottinghamshire innings.

"There was a key partnership between Bruce French and Richard Hadlee and Richard led a charmed life but they capitalised on our poor fielding. We had the chances to win and didn't take them.

**65**

"I'm sure that if any of those chances had been taken we would have gone on to win the match.

"Nottinghamshire went on to win by three wickets with three balls remaining, with Richard unbeaten on 70. But again we were so near and yet so far.

"During the season we'd played a lot of positive high-quality cricket to get us into a good position in the Championship and in two finals but ultimately we weren't able to take the prize in any of the major competitions.

"Inevitably it was difficult for us not to feel disappointed. I particularly felt for Geoff Cook as I felt he deserved success."

Ripley added: "David's innings against Yorkshire at Lord's in the Benson & Hedges Cup final displayed both quality and grace.

"It was memorable, not just for its execution but also for the fact that one shot into the crowd managed to hit my mum on the foot. To pick my mum out in a crowd of 25,000 takes some doing!

"Against Nottinghamshire in the NatWest final he took a bit of tap off Richard Hadlee.

"But you could never bet against him on the big occasions when he was well and truly fired up because he had this happy knack of being able to change a game by getting out some top cricketers!"

Coverdale revealed that the bitterness of that particular defeat was actually transformed into one of the abiding memories of his tenure at Wantage Road.

He said: "We enjoyed a very good day with bat and ball on the Saturday and most people thought we'd won it on the Saturday night when play stopped in probably the best conditions of the whole day.

"On the Monday, Richard Hadlee won the game single-handedly for Nottinghamshire but we somehow managed to drop him four times from five balls.

"One of the misses was by Rob Bailey at deep long-off. Rob had the catch lined up and all of a sudden the sun came out and took the flight of the ball out of his vision. He never even laid a hand on it. It was freakish.

"There was total silence in the dressing room at the end of that game and I felt sorry for Geoff Cook who clearly felt he was destined not to win a trophy. It was heart breaking.

"However we eventually got ourselves together and went for a few beers in the Abington public house once we'd got to Northampton, which to be honest we should have done after the semi! What was amazing was that a bunch of guys who had been so down a few hours earlier came together as a team again that night. Looking back it was actually one of the great memories."

Capel had a busy winter ahead of him and played his first overseas Tests for England in Pakistan, a tour racked by controversy following the infamous stand-off between the England skipper Mike Gatting and the late umpire Shakoor Rana.

He struggled in the face of some dubious umpiring decisions but held everything together to post 98 in the Karachi Test.

He finally got to grips with the mastery of leg-spinner Abdul Qadir and Ripley said: "I felt for David when he just missed out on a century in the Test series in Pakistan.

"I think I recall Jack Russell having his camera ready in the pavilion, ready to capture his maiden Test century.

"It was a shame he fell two runs short. It will always be a case of what might have been and, knowing Capes, he would have stewed on ending up two runs short.

"He had proved that he was a more than useful bowler, to the extent that his all-round abilities got him an England call.

"But the England selection sidetracked him a little because they wanted a line-and-length bowler. **67**

"That wasn't really Capes. He was at his best charging in at a good pace, a wicket-taking bowler."

Coverdale felt that the 1987 history book should not judge Northamptonshire harshly.

He said: "Although we lost the two domestic finals, we did brilliantly that year. It was one of the best years in the club's history, even though ultimately we had nothing to show for it.

"One of the main reasons for that was the fact that Capes was having a very good season.

"David made his Test debut in 1987 and went on to play 15 Test matches for England, all bringing with them an unfair burden of expectation.

"To me it appeared that David naturally put pressure on himself to succeed, there was all the talk of the next Botham in the background and, when selected, he found himself in an England dressing room with little managerial support – certainly compared to what is available these days.

"He had to go out and do his job, sometimes not knowing exactly what his job was.

"Many players in that dressing room promoted their self-interest above the team's interest and Capes had to find his way through all of this pretty quickly.

"The England team in those days wasn't the greatest of set-ups to be part of.

"Some of the cricketers selected felt they were nothing more than sticking plaster, not valued or supported and easily discarded.

"Team England is a much better place to be for Test cricketers nowadays.

"David didn't let himself down in Test cricket in any sense. Indeed he made a very good half-century on debut against Pakistan to get England out of the mire.

"He wasn't blessed with best fortune on the tour of Pakistan where he played under Mike Gatting, a captain he respected.

"But he did make a fine 98 in Pakistan, which turned out to be his highest Test score.

"I think if he'd have reached three figures on that occasion his international future may have turned out differently.

"A century would have given him a massive boost and released a lot of that pressure that surrounded him.

"If you get a Test century it is there on your record forever, you know you don't have to achieve that again."

The domestic season of 1988 beckoned and, on a personal level for a budding sports journalist, it was an exciting time.

I had been granted the opportunity to cover the fortunes of Northamptonshire cricket for the evening newspaper in Northampton, the Chronicle & Echo, where I had been working as a news and football reporter.

It promised to be a labour of love and also a testing challenge not least as I knew that the chap I was taking over from, a gifted and witty writer with an irreverent pen, would be a very hard act to follow.

Pete Clifton had an exceptional ability in writing 'outside the box' and his copy was always light and hugely entertaining.

It was a style I admired and could relate to and one which I wanted to perpetuate, if not mimic.

An introductory meeting with secretary manager Coverdale was successfully negotiated and my name was added to the club's hotel booking list for the long line of away matches.

And I was soon to be the proud owner of a pristine red averages book, the bright yellow Wisden Cricketers' Almanack and the key tome in any cricket writer's armoury – the Playfair Cricket Annual.

The short hop to Oxford for the traditional warm-up game at The Parks beckoned and, as was also tradition in the middle of April, it was bloody freezing.

Goodness knows why a hardy band of cricket lovers chose to turn out at the university ground at all in those temperatures... but they did.

There wasn't much to write home about apart from the breaking news that a certain Australian fast bowling legend would be coming to play for Northamptonshire the following month.

The Benson & Hedges match with Yorkshire at Headingley was washed out but it represented my first introduction to some good sturdy Yorkshire folk – the five-strong army of writers covering the fortunes of the White Rose.

And the introduction ingrained an extreme fondness for Yorkshire and its cricketing history, which would develop as the years progressed.

Clifton had heavily marked my card as to the aggressive attributes of the wildcat among the notorious Tyke press corps, a formidable journalist by the name of Martin Searby – commonly and menacingly referred to by just his surname, Searby.

But the leader of the pack was the experienced Yorkshire Post writer John Callaghan (Cally), seemingly inseparably flanked by David Warner (Plum) of the Bradford Argus – the current Cricket Writers' Club president - Robert Mills (Freddie) of the Hull Daily Mail and David Hopps (Hoppsy) of the Yorkshire Evening Post.

I was introduced to the whole group by my travelling companion and local newspaper oppo Steve Harrison (Tubs), who was the cricket writer for the Evening Telegraph based in Kettering.

Yorkshire had comfortably the largest travelling press contingent on the county cricket circuit.

But little Northamptonshire also fared reasonably well in this respect, most counties being represented by only one scribe away from home and some counties had no journalist cover away from base. **70**

The lack of cricket on a rainy few days in Leeds meant social time well spent and although I had not yet actually seen any meaningful cricket, I had already become attuned to the daily rhythm of life as a cricket writer away from home turf.

My first decent chunk of cricket unfolded in a still cold late April and in one of the game's least glamorous outposts – Grace Road in Leicester.

And yes the good old NCG was also far from glamorous. But then again it was home.

The fact that cricket matches at Northampton could not get underway until May, once the Northampton Town football team (nicknamed the Cobblers) had finished churning up the outfield, made the County Ground interesting. If not glamorous.

I actually liked Grace Road, probably because it retained some exciting memories as a youngster following the Tudor Rose in the enemy Foxes lair.

Not least the thrilling derby Nat West Trophy quarter-final in 1981 when Northamptonshire triumphed en route to Lord's on a baking hot day.

That was far from a routine outcome against Leicestershire as the Foxes almost always retained the upper hand over their neighbours Northamptonshire... a similar hold to the one their rugby team Leicester Tigers has had over the Northampton Saints.

But there was one thing reassuringly familiar about that game in 1981.

County medium-pacer Tim Lamb dismissed the England starlet David Gower. And yes it was lbw! Lamb dines out on his famous 'bunny' but, skipping forward seven years, a more familiar outcome saw Northamptonshire walloped by an innings and 51 runs.

It enabled me to dash home to indulge my two other loves, watching the aforementioned Cobblers in their quest for promotion and, in the evening, the Eurovision Song Contest from Dublin.

The Eurovision winner that year was a Canadian songstress by the name of Celine Dion. Who went on to do pretty well. Not so bad, as Searby may have said...


## HOLDING OUT FOR A HERO?

The beginning of May was ushered in with Northamptonshire still awaiting its first victory of the campaign and excitedly holding out for a hero?

Well, one arrived and for yours truly they did not come much more heroic than this.

As a cricket-mad youngster, I loved tuning in to the Ashes series Down Under and hanging on Alan McGilvray's every word!

In those days I knew the names of all the Aussie cricketers off by heart.

And now Dennis Lillee was coming to play for Northamptonshire... somehow that didn't sound quite right. But it was happening.

And suddenly there he was, the embodiment of the mean and moody Aussie, flying the flag for Northamptonshire in what was nothing less than a sensational marketing coup for the club.

It was May 4, Star Wars Day, and we all hoped that 'maybe the fourth' would be with Northamptonshire for the season ahead.

It was raining and the nation's cricketing media had descended on Northampton.

The weather aside, Lillee manfully limbered up in the County Ground nets and took a lot of time out for the cameras.

Accompanied if memory serves me correctly with a promotional kangaroo provided by Lillee's visit sponsor Gestetner!                                    **72**

 SUBIACO, Western Australia
DENNIS LILLEE
Born: 18 July 1949
Northamptonshire: 1988 to 1989
RHB/RF

He had been tempted out of retirement by a job description which entailed sharing cricketing duties with the county's other overseas player Winston Davis, fulfilling promotional requirements for Gestetner and writing a column for the Daily Star, ghosted by the Star's cricket man Ted Corbett.

The following day saw the first home match of the season and Lillee was named in the Northamptonshire side for the Championship game against Gloucestershire, ensuring another media outpouring into the County Ground's tiny press box usually reserved for two reporters and Daily Telegraph writer Mike Carey's dog.

The national boys were to be out of luck on day one – following a rain delay, Northamptonshire had the audacity to bat and the great man was holed up in the pavilion.

But the following day their luck was in, Lillee taking a wicket with his eighth ball in a contest against Gloucestershire which was particularly compelling as it pitted Lillee against his compatriot and fellow West Australian, Terry Alderman, who was leading the line for the visitors and at that time a fixture in the Test side.

Alderman, like Lillee, was born in Subiaco, Western Australia, seven years separating them.

Lillee got one over young Alderman, taking 6-68 in the final innings of his debut game and setting up Northamptonshire's first four-day win of the season, by a margin of 49 runs.

**73**

The story could not have been better scripted and Lillee, buoyed by this early success in favourable seam conditions, joined up for the next stop on the Northamptonshire roadshow – the unlikely cricketing outpost that is Darlington!

The old Feethams ground in Darlington was better known for football matches rather than cricketing contests but here it was hosting the Minor Counties for a Benson & Hedges Cup fixture.

The gloomy weather had dissipated on the long journey north and the County Durham sunshine belted down.

A routine win was achieved but the journos, atop their perch on the pavilion roof with a bird's eye view of proceedings, had spotted that Lillee, who had been given the match off, was being kept busy in the field of promotions and public relations.

The Australian was naturally proving a big draw and county skipper Allan Lamb – embarking upon his Benefit Year had spotted a public relations opportunity of his own.

Lamb felt that he would clearly benefit from sending the great man out into the crowd on bucket collection duties.

And Lillee generously obliged, spending a good hour or so walking around the boundary edge rattling a bucket, glad handing spectators and signing autographs.

This set the tone for his stay at Northamptonshire. He proved to be a fantastic ambassador for the game of cricket, as much off the field as on it.

And he was a tremendous advocate for the skills and abilities of Rob Bailey and David Capel, both trying to establish themselves on the international scene.

Capel said: "Dennis instilled in me both confidence and belief and was proactive in talking up my international credentials.

"I remember an article that appeared from him in the Daily Star. He said this bloke is a good cricketer and should play for England and similarly he also pushed the claims of Rob Bailey.

"In the nets with Dennis, I performed to my maximum. He kept a close eye on my bowling, giving me advice along the way, and he was a great ambassador for us."

Coverdale added: "There was a little bit of a hangover following on from what had happened the previous year but Dennis Lillee arrived, cheered us up and was there for everyone who asked for advice and assistance. He was absolutely brilliant.

"He worked very hard with Capes on his game and made a tremendous impact off the field in an ambassadorial role. He made time for everyone which was astonishing as so many people made demands on him. It was a great lesson to learn."

Within days, a big Cup showdown arrived as Worcestershire rolled into Northampton with the likes of Ian Botham, Graeme Hick and Graham Dilley in their ranks.

With Northamptonshire fielding Lillee, Capel and Lamb, a titanic clash was in prospect and the press pack once more was out in force.

In the event, the contest was an anti-climax as Worcestershire cantered home by 125 runs and Botham edged the all-rounder tussle with Capel as the inevitable 'Who for England?' debate intensified.

Hick was voted man of the match – his stock was exceptionally high, having smashed 405 in a Championship match against Somerset at Taunton a week or so earlier – at that time the highest individual score in English cricket for 93 years.

Back in the Championship frame, the County Ground welcomed Warwickshire – another four-day match, one of a number being trialed in the programme as part of a future switch from three-day cricket to a longer form of the game.

On day one, the Bears batted and closed at 302-7, going on to post 415 the following day. Northamptonshire then replied with a paltry 170 all out and, following on, ended day two on 14-0.

On day three, Northamptonshire batted through to revive their fortunes and by the close were 331-8 – a lead of 86.

The tail wagged a little on the final day and Northamptonshire were finally dismissed for 363, setting their visitors a meagre 119 for victory.

The press boys were taking bets on what time the match would end and no-one really foresaw the drama to come.

Warwickshire were skittled out for 112 to give Northamptonshire a thrilling six-run victory.

With Lillee in town, the match evoked memories of the famous Botham and Willis game at Headingley in 1981, when England beat Australia in dramatic style also after following on.

It is thought that on this occasion Mr Lillee had decided not to have a bet on the outcome!

It is also thought that Dicky Rutnagur, of the Daily Telegraph, may well have done!

The match was widely recognised as a fantastic advert for four-day cricket, although the Warwickshire team may have been forgiven for not summing things up so enthusiastically.

The Oval in London was never one of my favourite haunts.

On my few visits there the vast arena would invariably be shrouded in gloom with very few good memories to reflect upon.

Without a large crowd in, its vastness would simply be overwhelming, the gloom seemingly all-enveloping.

One bright interlude from Northamptonshire's championship match in south London was a maiden century from opener Alan Fordham, whose career as a cricketer at the County Ground more or less co-incided with my tenure as cricket writer.

Fordham was a friendly, articulate and insightful cricketer from Bedford School, I had a lot of time for him and I was always pleased to see him do well. **76**

 BEDFORD, England
ALAN FORDHAM
Born: 9 November 1964
Northamptonshire: 1986 to 1997
Nickname: Forders
RHB/RM

*Alan Fordham – so unlucky not to play*
*for England, Keith Fletcher didn't rate him.*
*So that was that.*

A couple of days before the return Championship match with Leicestershire, the Chronicle & Echo newsroom came to a standstill late one afternoon when Lillee decided to pay an impromptu visit.

And it caused chaos!

Security was alerted after an unidentified vehicle rocked up and parked squarely across the trade entrance to the building.

The vehicle had blocked the route for the large tankers delivering ink and paper to the printing presses in those days housed on the newspaper's Northampton site.

All hell was let loose but the Lillee charm offensive was quickly turned on and no further action was taken as he gave an interview to the newspaper and met the editor and newsroom chiefs.

The deputy news editor of the day, the newspaper's rugby writer Terry Morris, cheekily ventured as to whether Lillee could spare a couple of hours to turn out for the Chron cricket team, the Spartak Pinkos.

Lillee politely declined and quickly changed the subject but the thought of Lillee bowling on Northampton's notorious Racecourse tracks? – now that would definitely have been a tale to tell!

Much like South African quickie Allan Donald doing local village side Overstone a favour and turning out for them some years later!

To end an eventful month of May for the Australian, Lillee's Northamptonshire career was effectively stalled big time courtesy of an awkward fall in the outfield in the Leicestershire game.

He was carried off the field with an ankle injury which was to keep him sidelined for several weeks.

Lillee's minder, Corbett of the Star, revealed that his man required an operation to repair torn lateral ankle ligaments.

To round off a despondent day, rain denied a possible victory for Northamptonshire on the final afternoon.    **78**

The Yorkies were in town at the start of June and, as is mostly the case when Northamptonshire and Yorkshire meet, there was a row.

Stand-in county skipper Wayne Larkins, with the sanction of captain Cook, agreed to use the same strip for the Yorkshire visit that had been used against Leicestershire.

Yorkshire soon found themselves in trouble, the pitch was reported to Lord's and the travelling press – all five of them – had a field day.

Searby and company were in top form and quietened down only when Northamptonshire, replying to Yorkshire's 155, were bowled out 25 runs behind. In the event the match was drawn, the weather again playing its part.

Next stop Taunton and, on a breezy first day, a little weather lore greeted me from the press box – 'if you can't see the Quantocks it's raining, if you can see the Quantocks it's going to rain.' Great!

The weather however behaved itself reasonably well, enough for Northamptonshire to secure a seven-wicket victory early on the final day to compensate a couple of near misses in the weeks beforehand.

Taunton is a lovely spot to watch cricket, the ground has a nice feel to it and it's only a short walk into the lovely town centre.

The Daily Telegraph's David Green, formerly of Lancashire and Gloucestershire, had made the short trip from his Bristol home for this game and kept the press box humorously regaled with his various tales of derring-do, both on and off the field.

And it was an entertaining first evening at the Deane Gate Hotel close to the M5, which ended with Nick Cook holding court in the hotel kitchen and Larkins spending a large chunk of the evening under a table.

Northamptonshire had a reputation of being one of county cricket's more sociable teams and Taunton and the West Country air inevitably brought out the best in them!   79

Northamptonshire drew with the West Indian tourists at Northampton and then made the short journey down the M1 to take on Middlesex at Wardown Park, Luton, as much a home match for the visitors as it was for Northamptonshire.

Luton usually produced a quick and true batting strip – there wasn't much in it for the bowlers and this match too ended in a draw.

But no-one really imagined the shock horror scenario about to unfold as the roadshow took a NatWest Trophy turn to the cricketing backwater of Boughton Hall in Chester.

The scorecard read as follows: Northamptonshire (1987 finalists) 161 all out; Cheshire (inspired by the former England batsman Barry Wood) 163-9.

Cheshire won by one wicket.

It was a humiliation for Northamptonshire cricket and for captain Cook, still struggling to come to terms with the twin Lord's disasters the year before, probably one setback too far.

A photo in the newspaper the following evening pictured Cook as a distant and forlorn figure on the balcony. The time had come to move on.

On the eve of the Championship fixture against Nottinghamshire at Trent Bridge, I finally caught up with young all-rounder Duncan Wild.

Wild and I had been schoolmates at Northampton School for Boys where Wild, as the outstanding cricketer in the school, was earmarked for greatness at a very tender age.

My abiding cricketing memory of him at school was when my form team drew Wild's form in the lunchtime cricket competition.

I can't remember whether we batted first or second, just that 'batting' would suggest we land bat on ball. The term 'missing' may have been more appropriate.

I do remember squaring up to this lithe blond-haired cricketing dynamo and just watching the ball fizz past the bat in a blur. And he wasn't even trying that hard.          **80**

And what I clearly remember from that lunchtime mismatch was that Mr Extras was our top scorer. And that we lost the match. Comfortably.

Twenty wickets fell on the first day at Trent Bridge, courtesy of another Nottingham pitch specially prepared by that groundsman of legend, Ron Allsopp.

Northamptonshire were blown away after folding on the last day, with Cook critical of a pitch which he felt was 'nearly dangerous.'

A home Championship match with Lancashire saw the Red Rose on top on the first day, with Pakistani paceman Wasim Akram in command.

The Sports Pink that evening ran the headline 'Brownwash' in acknowledging Akram's seven-wicket haul - Akram took exception to it, although he did not raise an official complaint.

Those were the days when politically incorrect headlines were by and large still deemed acceptable.

An oft-quoted favourite in Chronicle & Echo circles concerned the headline that accompanied Northampton Town football team's 1-0 win at Orient with a goal from forward Ian Benjamin – the headline read 'Benji finds a chink in the Orient'…

And I wished I'd been around for a draw between Derby County and Northampton Town – 'Rams held by the Cobblers'…

As a cub reporter though there are some things you learn quickly – never leave obscenities or profanities in your copy or catch lines, no matter how funny it may seem to you at the time.

This is why it wasn't clever to attribute the word 'bollocks' to Allan Lamb in a preview of his Benefit match, even though he did use the word but in what context I cannot accurately recall.

I thought that the word would actually be taken out by a sub-editor who would see the funny side. Wrong!          **81**

Lo and behold, it appeared in the preview story in lurid black and pink technicolour, albeit in something like paragraph 23, missed by the sub-editor, who probably hadn't read that far and consequently didn't see the funny side.

And unsurprisingly the 'bollocks' swiftly became a 'bollocking!'

Lamb's benefit would prove to be a lucrative affair - more of that anon - but the coffers would not be boosted by his County Ground Benefit match against Yorkshire, which was washed out.

My first introduction to the waterside of the fair city of Bristol was soon forthcoming.

It is fair to say that many of the county players saw the trip to Bristol as a social event spanning three days of carousing interspersed with a little bit of cricket here and there.

Even now, visits to Bristol prompt happy memories of tired days, long nights and copious amounts of alcohol and frivolity.

Rain washed out day one and, no sooner had I sobered up after a heavy opening night, it was down to the Bristol Clipper and a nearby wine bar in the company of most of the team.

This had no effect on Wayne Larkins and Allan Lamb who both scored stylish centuries at the Nevil Ground, Lamb's the fastest of the season to date.

Another highlight that day was the appearance of a pair of underpants fluttering from the Northamptonshire flagpole, clearly hoisted aloft to celebrate the batsmen's considerable achievements.

But which batsman did said pants belong to? The prank had all the hallmarks of court jester Lamb but he resented the inference that he was responsible.

So much so that he marched over to the press box and was adamant in telling the assembled hacks that the underpants belonged to Larkins! **82**

An evening visit to the Old Porthouse set up a thrilling final day with Northamptonshire setting their hosts 349 to win in a one-innings shoot-out. It went to the wire and Gloucestershire finally succumbed at 348, just one run short.

The momentum did not carry into the next three-day game away at Derbyshire where I had been forewarned about the infamous Derby ring road but, no matter, I soon got hopelessly lost and the pentagon roundabout leading to the ground swiftly took on dodecahedron proportions!

I finally staggered into the press box, late, and that too proved to be quite an experience from which I still haven't quite recovered.

'11am, Championship' uttered a voice from within and, with both my timekeeping and then the neatness of my averages book and press box etiquette under scrutiny, it all represented a testing introduction to the Derbyshire press boys.

The three wise men were Gerald Mortimer, the sharp-eyed cricket and football writer for the Derby Evening Telegraph, Neil Hallam – Daily Telegraph writer – and the local freelance Nigel Gardner.

A fearsome trio who ran the Yorkshire five very close in terms of their critical cricketing insight, their effortless humour and their clear determination not to suffer fools gladly.

The schoolmasterly presence of Mortimer kept everyone on their toes inside and outside the box.

You had to feel sorry for any hapless youngster ('move away') or older spectator ('you should know better') who would happen to block his view of the game.

Hallam's acidic asides were a joy (but only if they weren't aimed at you) and Gardner complemented them both beautifully.

Derbyshire's Great Dane, Ole Mortensen, rolled over Northamptonshire on the final day and inconsistency continued to be very much the order of the day.

# WHITE HORSE ON A RED BACKGROUND

The three-day game against leaders Kent at Northampton marked a star turn from Telegraph writer Mike Carey's companion golden Labrador, who took a clear liking to hoovering up any sandwiches and stray ice creams that a careless journo may have happened to have left lying around in a bag or on the table.

Kent won by one wicket on the final day, continuing their push for title glory, and their visit brought to mind the Northamptonshire public announcer, 'Ramshackle' Ron Staniford, who on the morning of each home match would address the two men and a dog in the County Ground in revered Arlottesque tones.

It was worth listening to Ron every morning – announcing the teams and the captain, promoting Bill Darker's away coach trips and all matter of other froth.

He excelled himself on the opening day of one home match against Kent when he made reference to the visiting team's flag, as he routinely did, flying from the top of the scoreboard.

He said, the Arlott burr in full effect: "If you look at the scoreboard, there you can see the flag of Kent, which is a white horse on a red background. Now, I've often wondered why it is a white horse on a red background, if there is a man of Kent in the ground who can tell me why it is a white horse on a red background I would really like to know."

Sure enough a man of Kent was pointed in the direction of Ron's announcer's booth next to the press box.

The man of Kent found Ron and said: "Ere, are you the bloke who wants to know about the Kent flag?

Ron replied: "Yes, can you tell me why it is a white horse on a red background?

Man of Kent: "Well let's put it this way, it's a white horse on a red background because if it was a red horse you wouldn't be able to f****** see it!"  **84**

That was Ron put straight but I'm not sure whether he saw the funny side!

Enquiries about other county flags from that moment on were not too forthcoming!

Sussex were up next, skittled for 118 on day one with Winston Davis achieving career-best figures of 7-52 and David Ripley taking six catches behind the stumps.

By now, Rob Bailey was nearing 1,000 runs for the season and Allan Lamb was once more leading the way with the bat against the touring West Indians.

Lillee matched up against Imran Khan in the Sunday game, which the county won, but the Championship affair petered out into a bore draw.

Capel had taken the other three wickets in the Sussex first innings and Ripley said: "I enjoyed keeping to Capes. He bowled at a good pace and could get the ball to swing both ways.

"His natural instinct was to attack at all times and he would often suggest to me that I should stand wider when keeping off his bowling.

"My view was to keep a more narrow line but he felt that by doing so I was losing ground.

"My counter argument was that by not standing too wide would allow me to cover more ground. We kicked that one around a few times over a pint!

"But I picked up a lot of edges off Capes and didn't mess up too many so I think we were both happy with the way things worked out!

"I picked up a lot of catches that year but was lucky to be paired up with a good bowling attack.

"When Winston found his game he would get the ball to swing a little late and there were plenty of catches popping up to me and the slip fielders."

The month of July ended with a trip to lovely Worcester and a stay in the cathedral city's Diglis Hotel, tucked away by the River Severn.

**85**

I arrived on the evening before the game to something of a mutiny – the players were already in situ and extremely unhappy that the hotel rooms were not up to standard.

The team did not stay in the most expensive hotels, as a rule they were comfortable and of good quality.

But on this occasion the Diglis did not pass muster and a transfer was hastily arranged to the Giffard Hotel in the city centre, the county's usual hotel of choice.

The nearby Severn View was not on the radar, as some years previously there had been an incident when one of the team's fast bowlers somehow managed to crash through a wall into a neighbouring room!

Lillee was in the Northamptonshire side at New Road, fast bowler Mark Robinson was in form but the day belonged to the prolific Graeme Hick who hit 132 out of the home side's first-day total of 321-5.

It was that evening that I asked Lillee his opinion on the merits of run machine Hick compared to the world's greatest batsman Viv Richards.

Lillee looked incredulous, managed a facial expression somewhere between a snort and a smile and said that it was not possible to compare the two.

His view was that Richards had proved himself a master batsman at the highest level, while Hick had so far only managed to flat-track bully a few county attacks.

He added that any comparison could only be made once Hick was embedded within the international cricket scene – and he doubted that anyone would ever better Richards.

The Worcester ground is a particular favourite of mine and so too the L'Aroma Greek restaurant, where the meze was to die for – for me and Tubs Harrison, it was the top eating place on tour!

Another tame draw resulted but not after a quite extraordinary end to the second day. Worcestershire had declared on 362-6 and had promptly dismissed Northamptonshire for 191, trailing by 171. **86**

Routinely, this would have required the county to follow on and everyone in the ground was surprised when Cook actually led his team back onto the field.

Only for home skipper Phil Neale to chase after Cook with his team behind him, far from happy.

Neale remonstrated with Cook during a long stand-off that he had asked Northamptonshire to bat again so why wasn't this being observed?

Cook argued back, saying that he had received no such instruction and had therefore assumed that Worcestershire wanted to build on their first-innings lead.

The umpires were unable to resolve the situation that evening but when the final day got underway, Northamptonshire, as expected, indeed ended up following on.

Wellingborough School was another much-loved venue and at the time a regular home fixture in August.

The County Ground press box would uproot down the A45 for three days and base itself by the beautiful old pavilion on the school ground.

I was back in the fold after a short break and straight to the action in Wellingborough.

No different when, as a news reporter, a punishment for having had the audacity to take some time off would invariably result in you being exiled to the Wellingborough news office or, even worse, solitary confinement in a windowless room in Daventry!

Wellingborough School was different though - Glamorgan were the visitors, the sun shone, and Lamb hit a quickfire century to bring a much-needed victory.

From now on in there were only two away games to go, the first being a four-day outing against Yorkshire by the seaside at Scarborough.

Here began my love affair with this quintessential English seaside resort, which was explored from the team base at the St Nicholas Cliff Hotel.

The sun shone brightly in the early September sky and Yorkshire enjoyed a good first day on a good batting strip, with a fair crowd flocking into the amphitheatre which gives Scarborough its atmospheric edge.

My first visit to the press box was eagerly awaited by the Yorkshire mafia press corps, who traditionally note whether or not newcomers have the nous to find their way into their crow's nest.

It isn't easy, because the entrance to the stairs to the press box actually required you entering the ladies' toilet!

I can't remember whether or not I passed the test first time but I did make it in and quickly renewed acquaintances which were established at Headingley early in the season.

Another sociable spot, there was plenty going on and, with the Yorkshire press lads also on a stopover, the trip was a lot of fun.

Cook scored a career-best 203 against his home county, Larkins was left at home and, unsurprisingly, a high-scoring match ended in a draw with seemingly as much action off the field as on it.


## THE MARCH OF OLD FATHER TIME

There was not much respite before the final Championship game of the season, against Essex at Chelmsford.

Northamptonshire started the match well but Essex hung in there and profited from a sporting declaration on the final afternoon.

There was a moment of amusement at the close of the county's first innings which saw Nick Cook and 'rabbit' Robinson at the crease.

Robinson, famous for a string of ducks, chose the moment to score his highest score in first-class cricket – 19 not out.                                                          **88**

But the Essex scoreboard operator clearly couldn't believe what he or she was seeing and chalked up all of Robinson's runs to Cook!

There followed a teapot moment from an irate Robinson who waited patiently for the scoreboard to be corrected!

On the final day, Lillee's final match for Northamptonshire saw him entertain the Chelmsford crowd by engaging in a little banter with then England captain Graham Gooch.

With Essex on a victory chase, Lillee had sneaked out an Old Father Time mask and, at the end of his run up, put it over his face and ran up to bowl to Gooch.

But Gooch had made it quite clear to the umpires that he wouldn't be walking if they called time on him when Old Father Time was bowling!

Gooch insisted that a dead ball be called in such an eventuality!

The crowd saw the funny side and Gooch survived the march of time to see his side home - but not before opening partner John Stephenson became Lillee's final wicket in first-class cricket!

Lillee had obviously invested in a number of face masks... that much became apparent a few days later following the club's end-of-season lunch at the Carlsberg Brewery in Northampton.

The day of the dinner had begun with Cook announcing his stepping down as county skipper and this concentrated minds at the function.

A smorgasbord was coupled with copious pints of lager and by the end of the dinner these had become depth charges with the addition of shots of aquavit.

All the players were pretty boozed up by the time they headed to the Coach House hotel in the afternoon to continue drinking, this time a stag celebration to mark wicketkeeper David Ripley's wedding the following weekend. **89**

This resulted in more lager and champagne, a difference of opinion between old pals Cook and Larkins and also the sight of Lillee, this time in a Michael Jackson mask, weaving along the busy Kettering Road, stopping traffic and singing to motorists on their way home in the rush hour!

I went into the office the next morning still the worse for wear and later discovered, neatly placed in the back of the car, Lillee's Groucho glasses and Cook's drinking jacket!

Cook said: "Captaining Northamptonshire brings back many happy memories, it was good fun taking charge of a team of fun characters and talented cricketers.

"We played attacking, competitive cricket with a smile but lacked the ability to finish things off when it mattered.

"The two domestic Cup finals in 1987 are a stark reminder of that and those two games have stayed with me to this day."

Cook enjoyed captaining the young Capel. He said: "David was a very intense cricketer and was often the butt of jokes in the dressing room.

"He could maybe have relaxed more at times, but I firmly believe that this intensity was an integral part of his make-up and drove him on to achieve what he did.

"Do I think he would have been a better cricketer with a more laid-back approach? I don't think so, no, certainly not.

"It's a shame that David never had the opportunity to play Twenty20 cricket because I think his game would have been ideally suited to the discipline.

"I would have loved to have seen a Northamptonshire Twenty20 side including Capes, Allan Lamb and Wayne Larkins. It wouldn't have been dull!

"A talented batsman with the ability to score quickly, an effective medium-fast bowler and an athletic fielder, David was a very good example of an authentic three-dimensional cricketer."

Bailey was selected for the winter tour to India but there was no place for Capel or Nick Cook.                    **90**

The tour was eventually cancelled because of the South African links of some of the tourists, Bailey included, and Northamptonshire's big number three thought that this probably spelled the end of his Test career but he needn't have worried on that score.

Lillee was keen to help Capel find a path into the England team and when I caught up with Lillee in Perth again in November 2012, all of 23 years later, he reflected on the eager-to-please all-rounder that he had encountered at the County Ground in the late 1980s.

He said: "At that time there was the inevitable comparison between Capes and Both. David was certainly no Botham, but then again nor was anyone else.

"There was only one Botham and comparing any all-rounder to him was only going to put extra pressure on that person, be it David or Phil DeFreitas, Chris Lewis, Derek Pringle and no doubt several others.

"When I arrived at the club I saw a very capable all-round cricketer whose batting, at that stage, was more advanced than his bowling.

"David wasn't a relaxed cricketer, he was very intense and tight and this tended to affect him at times.

"The tension he experienced could be a little bit too great and impacted upon the control he would have over his own game.

"He wasn't a natural but always tried very hard to get where he wanted to be. He was eager to learn anything and everything about fast bowling and I passed on whatever I could. He was always willing to listen and he always wanted to advance himself.

"He was a great team player. I found that he was able to relax more easily over a beer at the close of play and I enjoyed his company.

"Sadly, I don't think he fulfilled the potential that he had. I felt he had the skills to go further in the game than he did.

**91**

"If he had concentrated more on his batting I think that, potentially, he was Test standard on that basis alone.

"I saw David as something of a Bob Woolmer, not necessarily a number three bat but a very capable batsman who could turn his arm if needed.

"In those days however it was more realistic to look at cricketers with all-round potential and that was how David was always regarded.

"Going back to the Botham question, I think it was easier for Both to fit in as an all-rounder in a strong Somerset attack than it was for David to fit in at Northamptonshire.

"The attack at Northamptonshire was not up to the Somerset standard of some years before so it was harder for David.

"It ended up as a lot more work for him and that, ultimately, worked against him.

"But of course any cricketer worth his salt and with potential will have the ambition to represent his village, his town, his county or state and ultimately his country.

"That alone brings with it extra pressure on top of the pressure of being tagged the next Botham.

"David has made a very good coach, both for fast bowling and batting and he has sent some players my way to the Academy that I run in India.

"If David had been Australian, would it have turned out different for him as international cricketer?

"I don't know. What I do know is that he would have had less matches to play in Australia than in England and, as a Shield cricketer, he would have had more time to concentrate on playing his game to the best of his ability.

"He would have had ample time to gee himself up between matches and be given the space to get himself properly motivated.

"In England he had more games to play and he would get worn out much more quickly.                                    **92**

"Multiply that schedule over many seasons and I think it is inevitable that an individual's concentration or interest in the task in hand would wane.

"These days, the schedule is fuller all over the world, certainly since the advent of Twenty20, but giving contracts to Test cricketers has helped focus their attention more effectively than was the case 30 or so years ago when they did not exist.

"This might explain why Australia are no longer the dominant force in world cricket that they were for a staggering two decades since the late-1980s.

"To be the top team in the world for so long was an amazing achievement but of course a great deal was down to the performances of some extraordinary cricketers around at the time.

"Any team with Shane Warne and Glenn McGrath in full effect would be nigh on impossible to beat.

"And then the likes of Ricky Ponting, Adam Gilchrist and Matthew Hayden kept the flag flying, to such an extent that a player of the calibre of Mike Hussey could not get a look in for a very long time.

"He is known as Mr Cricket, a superb batsman who will be missed by Australia.

"When he could not get into the Test side he was not alone in feeling frustrated as Australia had tremendous quality in reserve in all areas of the team.

"The measure of any outstanding sports team is the quality in reserve keeping those in the first team on their toes at all times.

"Australia no longer has the depth of quality in the ranks, so it may be some time before they go from being good to great once again."

At the County Ground in 1989, after much deliberation and speculation, the club's best player Allan Lamb was finally unveiled as the new club captain.

An early indication of our developing professional relationship came in response to a light-hearted question I asked Lamb after the serious stuff was over.

I asked him whether it would now be hard to adapt to a new and responsible role for someone who liked to lark around? Was umpire Dickie Bird's newspaper now safe from being set on fire, for example?

An innocuous knockabout question, or so I thought, but Lamb's responded with a po face and a straight bat and simply said: "I thought you came to ask about cricket?"

For my money, with Lamb still in the England frame, Nick Cook may have been a better captaincy bet from within the dressing room candidates.

As one national commentator put it, making Allan Lamb captain of a team is akin to letting Billy Bunter loose in the tuck shop.

But Lamb pressed his case hard and had the ear of those with influence at Wantage Road.

Capel summed up the Lamb captaincy: "There were fewer England distractions as time went by and in 1995, his final year with the club, he had become a very good captain indeed.

"I found Lamby was a very principled cricketer –he enjoyed having fun and played cricket with a smile on his face.

"He was a cavalier cricketer and this fitted what I like to call the Northamptonshire spirit well.

"His brand and style was attractive, his cricket expressive and entertaining.

"Under his captaincy the side sought to win every game and he was prepared to risk defeat with that philosophy. During the 1990s, even if we didn't win every game we certainly won a high percentage."

Capel felt that several new recruits fitted in with the club's quest to always play in an attacking and entertaining manner. **94**

TREBANOS, Glamorgan, Wales
GREG THOMAS
Born: 12 August 1960
Northamptonshire: 1989 to 1991
RHB/RF

He added: "We signed West Indian fast bowler Curtly Ambrose and also Greg Thomas from Glamorgan, considered the fastest white bowler around.

"I thought Greg was a good signing for us and felt that he would take some of the pressure off my workload.

"I had been experiencing increasing problems with my back and his arrival, together with the introduction of Curtly Ambrose, was not only beneficial for the team but helped me greatly.

"Greg was seriously quick and swung it away late. He certainly added value in the dressing and loved to banter.

"He and Winston Davis had both been team-mates at Glamorgan and Greg would regularly wind Winnie up about all manner of things.

"We also signed Nigel Felton, an experienced batsman from Somerset who had previously been on Kent's books and who was to prove another very good addition to the side.

"Felts went on to forge a very good opening partnership with Alan Fordham.

"Felts had been around the block a little and he hadn't had an easy time of it.

"He was part of some big dressing rooms at Kent and then Somerset, from where he was released. He was a good addition to our camp, he had some pretty astute views on the game."

Felton recalled: "When I was at Somerset, we played some counties twice and others only once and Northamptonshire always fell into the latter category. **95**

GUILDFORD, Surrey, England
NIGEL FELTON
Born: 24 October 1960
Northamptonshire: 1989 to 1994
Nickname: Felts
LHB/OB

*Nigel Felton – enjoyed his time with Northamptonshire, after a difficult time at Somerset, and now sits on the club's committee*

---

"My confidence had been shattered at Somerset but the lads were great, Nick Cook especially, and what struck me immediately was how different a club Northamptonshire was compared to Somerset.

"The dressing room at Taunton had imploded several years before.

"The legacy of that implosion was marked and it was such a relief to arrive at a club where there was no tension in the dressing room.

"You still had some excellent cricketers and very strong characters at Northampton, don't get me wrong, but they were much easier to be around and much more my type of people.

"I almost drifted to Northamptonshire, thinking that my career probably had only another year or so to run.

"I knew that Northamptonshire were looking to life after Geoff Cook and Wayne Larkins, but I also knew they were looking to bring in the likes of Alan Fordham and Neil Stanley.

"So I thought I would just be batting cover and it was no surprise when I started the 1989 season in the Second XI with Bob Carter to get me bedded in.

"I had previously captained Young England to Australia ten years previously and Bob had been my vice-captain so we knew a little bit about each other and got on well.

"But even at that early stage I was enjoying my cricket again and my time at Northampton was comfortably the most enjoyable time during my entire career, by a clear country mile.

"What I liked about Northamptonshire was that it was a down-to-earth club, just very easy going.

"The skipper Allan Lamb played a big part in that. He was a big personality but he could always laugh at himself and I liked that.

"And looking back, you had the likes of Capes, Mark Robinson and Wayne Noon in that dressing room, all of whom went on to make their mark in management and coaching.

"We didn't do much in my first year and at the end of it I still felt my future was very uncertain."

## FOR WHOSE BENEFIT?

The 1989 campaign began at Derby – it always seemed to be Derby in April or May, it always seemed to be bleak, it always seemed to be very cold.

The County Ground at Derby was probably the only ground on the circuit less welcoming than Northampton.

I suspect that the Midlands grounds trio of Northampton, Leicester and Derby would never be the choice of any discerning cricket writer, the regional exception of course being the Test class facilities at Nottingham's Trent Bridge.

There was nothing much to write home about as the match ended in a draw in arctic-like conditions.

An abiding memory of the final afternoon was of poor Winston Davis, not long back from the Caribbean, shivering on the boundary edge clad in three sweaters. His body language said it all.

The heater was on in the car as the roadshow navigated its way to Edgbaston, through rain and sleet, for a Benson & Hedges Cup battle against Warwickshire.

This was my first introduction to the Strathallan Hotel on the Hagley Road in Birmingham, always one of my favourite hotels on the circuit.

Lamb entertained, Northamptonshire won and it was swiftly on to Bristol for a Championship match against Gloucestershire.

And back to the Unicorn, another favourite resting place, and this time no problem with the directions to the hotel through the city from the M32.

A good start to the Championship campaign resulted augured well– a win by ten wickets - and Leicestershire were the first visitors to the County Ground.

A tight affair saw the visitors bowled out for 250 on the final day, setting Northamptonshire a very testing 276 to win in not much time.

What followed was a brutal display of batting from Lamb who took the Foxes attack apart, in particular the hapless Jon Agnew who managed a wry smile as the devastation unfolded.

The county hung on to win by one wicket, Lamb left the field to a standing ovation from both sides and all quarters and the bandwagon rolled on.

A Sunday win followed against Warwickshire and heralded a week which would turn out to be a very strange one indeed. I remember it very clearly.

Monday 8 May, a day off from the cricket which was spent enjoying the total peace and quiet of beautiful, unspoilt Fawsley, just outside the town of Daventry in the rural west of the county.

A real Northamptonshire gem, one-time home to Elephant Man John Merrick – do stop off if you are able to stop while passing through!

Tuesday 9 May – back to Benson and Hedges Cup action at the County Ground and Northamptonshire continued their winning streak with a comfortable win over Lancashire.

And you don't get to say that too often of you are a Steelbacks supporter!

Before that game, I'd written up a story about the results of Lamb's substantial £134,000 Benefit Year for the evening edition.

I thought nothing more of it but the following day was asked to phone secretary Coverdale, who ranted about the tone of the coverage given to Lamb's Benefit and that the story was given too high a profile.

Considering that Lamb's benefit was a quiet and understated affair - not! - I had to smile at that point!

Coverdale also passed on the message that Lamb was withdrawing co-operation from the newspaper.

Lamb's objection was that I had made fulsome reference to the fact that his Benefit Year had not been without controversy.                                               **99**

Events had been organised all over the country and there were many very irritated, beneficiaries in other counties who felt that Lamb had discourteously ridden roughshod over their own arrangements ... and that it just wasn't cricket.

Lancashire's John Abrahams was one case in point and Lamb's activities indeed were so far reaching that even HM Revenue & Customs had begun to take a keen interest.

Full support was forthcoming from my bosses at the Chronicle & Echo who stated the newspaper's case to the cricket club in no uncertain terms.

It could, and should, have been sorted out quickly. But the club chose to back its newly-elected captain and in the resulting stand-off it was going to be a sorry case of seeing who blinked first.

Lamb's truculence, in part, was later ascribed to annoyance that the Chronicle & Echo deputy sports editor Brian Barron had earlier in the year written an article which made reference to new signing Thomas's financial arrangements on joining Northamptonshire, which allegedly included a £20,000 signing-on fee.

Lamb meanwhile was making a clear statement with the bat and his early season form ensured his star was in the ascendancy.

This, allied with his undoubted strength of character and his close friendship with the club chairman Lynn Wilson, ensured that his views held sway.

The local newspaper was now also required to toe captain Lamb's line and, naturally enough, this did not go down well with the newspaper's editor Clive Hutchby.

He suggested it would be in everyone's best interests to change my flight booking to Scotland at the weekend, which had been organised with the club, and travel to the game independently.

Thursday 11 May – Northamptonshire were at home to Leicestershire in the Benson and Hedges Cup. Awkward! **100**

Lamb was again in fine form after a delayed start to the match and in the late afternoon I was summoned to Steve Coverdale's office where the mother of all rows exploded.

Not least, I was annoyed that the meeting had been called but that the club secretary then spent half the time watching the game and not addressing the matter in hand.

Coverdale insisted that an apology to Lamb should be forthcoming and I told him that would not be happening and that I expected him to speak to Lamb and ensure that normal service be resumed as quickly as possible.

At which point I stomped back to the press box and had to be calmed down by the avuncular Daily Telegraph writer Mike Carey, whose words of wisdom at that juncture were greatly appreciated.

Friday 12 May - The Leicestershire match finally fell foul to the weather but the sun was shining as I flew on my own some to Glasgow for the next one-day game with Scotland at Hamilton Crescent.

Awkward again for a young reporter, seemingly persona non grata with the players on the instruction of the captain, having to negotiate chance meetings in the corridors of the Crest team hotel in Argyle Street, where I had remained put!

Saturday 13 May – with the team out early on their way to the ground in their hired minibus, I thought it would be safe to enjoy a late breakfast at the team hotel, but this is where the fun and games began!

There weren't many diners in the breakfast room but one of them just happened to be Lamb, who had decided to sit out the game and was not with the team on the bus.

To compound the felony, having ordered a taxi for the ground, I was then asked by the hotel receptionist that another gentleman was going to the cricket and would I mind sharing?

I replied that this wouldn't be a problem but by now you can probably guess what happened next...                **101**

And so I was joined in the cab by Lamb for a journey across Glasgow, obviously not quite persona non grata enough for him to turn down a free ride. The small talk was very small but remained cordial and I paid the fare on arrival as Lamb went on ahead. A bizarre morning in Partick continued in the same vein as an expectant crowd waited for the Northamptonshire players to warm up on the field.

But they were late arriving at the ground, on account of the fact that their minibus driver had mistaken the instruction Hamilton Crescent for Hamilton, a nearby small town and footballing home of the Academical, and had taken the players on a merry Saturday morning tour of Lanarkshire!

The minibus eventually rolled in from its rural route but a slight delay did not hold up Northamptonshire by much, a nine-wicket win routinely secured.

The following Monday saw the arrival of West Indian quickie Curtly Ambrose at the County Ground. The club gave me permission to interview Ambrose but he wasn't saying a great deal. Then again he never did!

The Yorkshire mafia came to town for a four-day fixture and were keen to catch up on all the gossip – Yorkshire fixtures were never short of some sort of rumpus, usually Yorkshire flavoured, but this time they were pleased for once that the boot was on the other foot!

The mood was lightened with the Yorkies playing their 'Nelson' game – cash to be stumped up towards an end-of-season meal by a given nominee every time 111 appeared on the scoreboard or a wicket fell on that number.

On one of the days in the game the previous season, the hapless David Hopps was stung no less than four times!

But the interview ban was re-instated and the farcical situation persisted.

A meeting was arranged with me, my deputy sports editor Brian Barron, Coverdale and Lamb at the club offices at high noon the following day, when hopefully the whole issue would be put to bed.                                    **102**

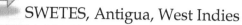

SWETES, Antigua, West Indies
CURTLY AMBROSE
Born: 21 September 1963
Northamptonshire: 1989 to 1996
Nickname: Amby
LHB, RF

*Curtly Ambrose – a distinguished West Indies career but initially found life difficult at Northampton*

Barron and I turned up at the requested time and Coverdale was in his office but there was no sign of Lamb, who had still not showed up by 2pm.

Barron was incandescent and made it clear to Coverdale that the gloves were now off and that the newspaper would be going into print about the whole affair, which so far had been kept under wraps.

Friday 19 May – the rumpus was headline news on both the news pages and sports pages and the county had refused a right to reply.

Word swiftly got out to the national press who promptly got stuck in and a siege mentality set in at Wantage Road.

Yorkshire were despatched before lunch on the final day and the time had come to hit the long road to Swansea, where secretary Coverdale was spotted arriving at the quaint St Helen's ground armed with a clutch of national and local newspapers.

On the playing front, Finedon leg-spinner Andy Roberts – as opposed to the Antiguan head-spinner and the Northampton yarn-spinner – had been named in the squad, which would undoubtedly wreak havoc with the complexity of the hotel booking system!

Late arrival Ambrose made his Northamptonshire debut in the valleys and took a wicket with his first ball in county cricket, dismissing Alan Butcher.

That evening, I ventured out with friends to the White Rose pub in Mumbles– a popular drinking hole on the visit to South Wales - for a few beers.

Several of the players were also in the pub and the news had clearly been digested.

To my relief, and to a man, they were very supportive of the newspaper's position.

The trip was lively and the game followed suit with Northamptonshire, having been set 305 for victory, collapsing horrifically to 60 all out.                              **104**

At one stage the county scorecard read 1-4 and then improved marginally to 6-5!

Back home there was silence from the cricket club and so the newspaper was forced to make a final ultimatum.

The editor told the club that they had until the end of the month to restore normal working relations – if not, the Chronicle and Echo and the Sports Pink would withdraw coverage of the club.

Former county captain Jim Watts voiced his support of the newspaper's position in an interview and the newspaper's postbag suggested that the club was in the wrong and should put things right.

But going into deadline day, Wednesday 31 May, there was still no word from the Wantage Road bunker.

The deadline day also happened to co-incide with a home tie against Kent in the quarter-finals of the Benson and Hedges Cup.

I was covering the match not really that interested in the county's progress, wondering if that day at the ground would be my last as a cricket reporter.

Late in the day, word came through that the ban had been lifted and that normality had been restored, although it would still take another month or so for the status quo to truly return in terms of regaining Lamb's full co-operation.

The beginning of June saw Lillee return to Northampton as non-playing motivator-in-chief, and he enjoyed himself on his first match on the tour which was away to Sussex on a sunny weekend in Hove.

I still vividly recall one quiet evening in the hotel bar being livened up by the larger-than-life than Aussie who hauled a ghetto blaster into the room and pumped out songs from one of his favourite bands, the Bee Gees no less!

Northamptonshire came close to winning and the match was marked by two milestones – Geoff Cook reaching 20,000 first-class runs and David Capel hitting two centuries in the match.

**105**

Capel said: "I couldn't put a foot wrong at this stage of the season. I was playing well at this stage of the season and with real confidence. I was actually singing to myself and in tune with my surroundings, I was so relaxed.

"I was probably at my peak here in all areas of the game. I was playing intuitively and loving every minute of it!

"Ned Larkins was captaining the side and it was an easy equation with him.

"On joining the club I learned a lot from him, not just about the art of playing the game but also about the philosophy of winning cricket matches – I enjoyed his brand of aggressive and colourful cricket."

The county then took a break from the domestic campaign to prepare for the tour match against Australia at the County Ground.

The match took an interesting dimension in that Lillee was seemingly up for playing for Northamptonshire against the Aussies.

Not surprisingly, this proved to be little more than considerable hype.

Interest needed to be built in a tourist fixture which no longer held the same allure as in previous years – although this was Australia, and a bloody good Australian team it has to be said!

Lillee took it easy, spending most of the time in conversation with Allan Border and keeping Merv Hughes in check!

Lamb got himself injured during the match and young all-rounder Tony Penberthy claimed a wicket with his first ball in first-class cricket, that of Mark Taylor!

The county rolled over meekly in the last innings to give the tourists a 272-run victory and, indeed, the charity game that followed the main event appeared a tad more competitive!

Next stop Southport in coastal Lancashire for a three-day meeting with the Red Rose.                        **106**

A national rail strike meant the roads were busy but the team were soon ensconced in the town's famous old Scarisbrick hotel and it turned out to be an entertaining three days – off the field, if not on it.

The press tent was ruled by the fearsome combination of Searby and Green (the Daily Telegraph cricket writer David Green).

Whenever these two got together it was never dull, Green affectionately referred to his old mate Searby as the 'Dewsbury porker' and the two of them held court for the duration of an unexciting game.

As often happens, when the match itself is tedious, entertainment was sought elsewhere and the luncheon refreshment on the second day in the club pavilion extended well into the second session.

Well, pretty much up to the tea interval if I recall correctly, although admittedly I may not have been in a position to do so.

A couple of gin and tonics had turned into a couple more and they were gentlemen's measures at that.

It got quite raucous at one stage and once the press party had tipped out of the pavilion, a little quiet time by the boundary edge was in order.

In fact, I may have fallen asleep for some of the final session.


## CURTLY RESPONSE!

Somerset were up next at Luton in neighbouring Bedfordshire and this was my first match at lovely Wardown Park in a professional capacity.

Northamptonshire finished 12 runs short of a 321 final-day target so were a little despondent as they hit the road for the first round NatWest Trophy tie with Suffolk at Bury St Edmunds.

On the Sunday, Leicestershire were the one-day visitors where Ambrose was determined to show off another string to his bow.

Felton said: "David Ripley had gone off injured and the bowlers were easily on top but this was the game in which Curtly volunteered to take Ripley's place behind the stumps!

"He was talked out of it but he wasn't very happy as he had kept wicket before and felt he could do a good job.

"We had to remind Curtly that the Leicestershire batsmen would be loving it if they were having a chat with him behind the stumps rather than squaring up to him as he ran in to bowl!"

The trip to charming East Anglian town Bury St Edmunds resulted in another late first night.

I remember hooking up with a group of lovely students in the bars and then, for some reason, buying them all a Chinese meal. And I don't even like Chinese food!

Having crashed out in the early hours, I then had to surface at 7am to write the previous day's match copy for a morning deadline and having skipped breakfast, which wasn't like me, I travelled to the Victory Ground feeling distinctly liverish.

After the Cheshire debacle of the previous year, Northamptonshire were nervously contemplating this hurdle against the minnows from Suffolk and, having won the toss, were also on the liverish side early on.

Having opted to bat first, they soon found themselves on a perilous 16-3 with Geoff Cook, Wayne Larkins and Rob Bailey all back in the pavilion.

A clearly agitated Coverdale emerged in the press area at this point, certain that lightning was about to strike twice.

Lamb and Capel, however, dug deep and got the ship back on course and the first-class county made hard work of a 32-run victory against the minnows after the game had run into a second day.

**108**

Coverdale said: "I remember this match for all sort of reasons. We'd lost to Cheshire the previous year and a poor start had me worrying that the same thing could happen again.

"We lost three quick wickets and could have collapsed. In fact at one stage the scoreboard showed that we were 4 for 3 wickets down.

"That four had been a thin edge past leg stump. We could so easily have been nought for 4!

"Suffolk played like Gods but we eventually got the better of them although it was hard work for us.

"The game ran into two days and at tea on day one the players went in for the scheduled break only to be turned away by the tea ladies who said they weren't ready!

"As the weather closed in, farce descended as one of the umpires John Holder clearly wanted to get the game going and finished and insisted it was okay to play.

"The trouble was that the groundsman had covered up the pitch and surrounds and gone home!

"We couldn't play on and would need the second day, but that presented problems for both us and Suffolk.

"Some of their players had other commitments on day two and couldn't return to play.

"And we had a problem with our hotel booking which meant that they couldn't accommodate all of us for a second night.

"So I spent a lot of the time on the phone finding alternative accommodation for some of the players in Bury St Edmunds and the surrounding areas.

"It came to a point where players were billeted all over East Anglia!"

Champions Worcerstershire came to town for a three-day match and made light work of Northamptonshire.

Botham was in good form but his manners deserted him on the Sunday outing at Tring Park in early July.    **109**

The Telegraph writer on a sunny afternoon in Hertfordshire was the upper-crust and eccentric ASR (Tony) Winlaw, who had been despatched by his newsdesk from his home in leafy Warwickshire to get a comment from Botham about all things England.

Winlaw set out to find his target but returned hastily back to base, quite offended that Botham had told him quite bluntly to f*** off.

Tring was the seasonal Sunday social outing for Northamptonshire, more often than not bringing with it sunshine and the Men's Singles Final on a hundred pitchside transistor radios.

The press barbecue was always the highlight, hosted by Tubs Harrison and his wife Rita, the products of their regular meat raffle supplying plentiful food for the large gathering of hungry hacks.

As the barbie got underway on this occasion, a sponsor tent nearby came into difficulty and threatened to deflate and engulf its honoured guests.

At which point a flapping Coverdale materialised, arguably generating enough hot air to get the thing back upright without too much difficulty!

Lillee joined in the fun and frolics by joining the press corps and instructing us all in how to serve up a proper Aussie barbie.

The final word however went to Winlaw, clearly not over his Botham experience, who observed Lillee turning the sausages and whispered to one of the gathering:

'That chap at the barbecue looks familiar, is it Keith Miller?!'

Back in the Championship, the match was naturally billed as 'Botham v Capel' and it was Botham who took the honours, taking 6-99 in Northamptonshire's first innings in which Capel scored one.

Botham went on to take 11 wickets in the game and went on to win a Test slot against the Australians. **110**

Former skipper Cook gave his view on the Botham and Capel comparisons.

He said: "There were a lot of people in the same boat as David when it came to the search for the next Botham.

"The likes of Derek Pringle, Chris Lewis and Phil DeFreitas were all mentioned in despatches.

"David was just driven, he wanted to be as good as he could be and he naturally wanted to play for England.

"But the next Botham? I seriously don't think David ever saw himself as that as it was other people, mainly those in the media, who were applying this label."

Ripley observed: "There was all the 'next Botham' stuff with David and a lot of other all-rounder cricketing hopefuls at the time.

"I don't think the national selectors were necessarily more preoccupied with finding an all-rounder when Capes was at his peak.

"It all depends who is around at the time. At one point, they looked at batsmen/wicketkeepers, then of course Freddie Flintoff came on the scene and you were back in 'Botham' territory.

"It's all about balance in a side, whether that is Northamptonshire or England.

"What Capes gave the side was that balance, in that we could bat and bowl with more depth.

"If one player can score you a stack of runs and take wickets as well then you've got it made."

The Worcestershire drama took on another twist on the final morning.

I took a phone call from my newsdesk asking me to get some info on an incident the previous evening at the riverside Britannia public house in Northampton.

"Botham had apparently got himself into a brawl with a punter.

"Not only that but Lillee had also been at the pub with Botham and was also involved.

**111**

Fortunately the Star's Ted Corbett got a handle on the story which enabled me to steer well clear, mindful of my still delicate predicament with the club at the time.

The NatWest Trophy dream was ended by Warwickshire at the County Ground at the quarter-final stage, by three wickets in front of a large crowd.

And so the calendar clicked around to August and the away Championship match with Yorkshire, played at Sheffield's picturesque Abbeydale Park ground.

The convivial atmosphere hit the ground running with most of the players in the bar of the team's Hallam Tower hotel, now no more, on the Friday evening.

With Searby and Green also in attendance, this wasn't going to be dull!

The terrible twins were in full effect from the off and the Northamptonshire batsmen had a ball on day one, Alan Fordham hitting 199 and Rob Bailey 98.

Fordham's arrival had been greeted with an 'ey up, it's Alan Boredom' and 'here comes A Block' from Green, who was hastily required to revise his opinion on meeting up with Fordham later that evening!

There was a considerable news frisson around this match in respect of who might be signing up for a tour to then still out-of-favour South Africa.

And a night at Sheffield's legendary Josephine's night club was kicked off with some of Northamptonshire's finest – Greg Thomas and Duncan Wild, no names no pack drill - shinning down a lamp post from the hotel on to the Manchester Road to avoid the long walk to the hotel entrance. No injuries reported fortunately!

A sluggish second day's play saw Yorkshire trying to bat their way back into the game.

Their progress however found no favour with Searby who loudly voiced his displeasure at the White Rose tactics on quite a number of occasions. **112**

And some of the Northamptonshire players were getting a little confused with their field positions as they responded to the hand signals from stand-in skipper Wayne Larkins... only to later realise that he had been actually been waving to his then girlfriend Debbie who was seated in the crowd!

A long day was lightened in the bar that evening with all the press boys doing their very best to perfect their very own Freddie Trueman impressions.

To the point that Green observed: 'You do realise that anyone walking into the bar and listening to us lot will think we've been let out into the community!'

After dinner there followed a leaving do for Yorkshire Evening Post writer David Hopps, who was on his way to report cricket for the nationals.

A suite was hired for the occasion, the hotel apparently quite happy to oblige.

There had been some doubt about their willingness to enter into such an arrangement as Searby had once got involved in a spat with the hotel manager, to the point that he was intent on dangling said manager out of a window!

The party started at 9.30pm and went on until 5.30am by all accounts, a mere five and a bit hours before stumps were due to be set for the final day's play.

I did not see it out to the death, returning to my room in already emerging daylight.

After a few snatched hours of sleep, and a little weary to say the least, I set out for the ground passing by two tea flasks which were standing guard on the desk at the hotel reception.

The flasks were intended for Searby and Green, traditionally early risers. Not on this day however...

Both turned up after the day's play had got underway – I was tempted to say '11 o'clock, Championship' but thought that discretion might be the better part of valour!

Just before lunch, a clearly struggling Green disappeared from the press box for some considerable time.                 **113**

Searby was getting worried about his mate but, following a cursory sweep of the ground with his trusty binoculars, the concern quickly turned to contempt when he spotted Green curled up on a bank, not far from the boundary rope, fast asleep!

Searby was not amused, jogging round the ground to unceremoniously rouse his dormouse pal from his slumbers.

Northamptonshire went on to claim a 42-run victory but their routine good fortune against Yorkshire was never routinely extended against Essex, and again so it proved in the next match at Colchester.

In many ways it was a difficult three days, with computer glitches and an upset stomach presenting unwanted distractions.

But the press tent at Castle Park did have its lighter moments, not least when a local character known simply as Rocky paid a visit to the freelance reporter Nigel Fuller and proceeded to uproot the telephone cables in the tent ensuring that all reporting lines went down.

Northamptonshire also went down by 120 runs following a contrived run chase before making the thankfully shorter trip to London to face Middlesex at Lord's.

More entertainment in the capital, this time provided by Lord's press box grandee Norman de Mesquita – for me the voice of BBC London cricket – Dicky Rutnagur of the Daily Telegraph, never known to hold back an opinion, and the Independent's Mike Carey!

Middlesex won both long and short matches, the Sunday featuring anti-apartheid protests outside headquarters and wee Jimmy Govan, the county's Scots off-spinner making a rare first-team appearance, not being allowed back into the Lord's pavilion because the attendants did not believe he was playing in the match!

With Lamb on Test duty, Larkins took over the reins for the home Championship match with Warwickshire which turned out to be nothing short of an embarrassment.     **114**

The 1988 match between the two counties was a classic – a tremendous ding-dong battle over four days.

The 1989 contest was all ding and no dong whatsoever and lasted little more than a day!

The first day saw Northamptonshire bowled out for 51 – their county's lowest first-class score since 1946 – Warwickshire were then dismissed for 191 and the county closed on 27-2 in their second dig.

A total of 22 wickets down on day one, it required just another eight to fall on day two to settle the match.

They all toppled before lunch, Northamptonshire all out for 109 and defeated by an innings and 31 runs.

To his credit, Larkins faced the press straight afterwards and put the shambles down to a 'loss of confidence'... which would not be helped by the impending return visit of Essex to the County Ground.

However, Northamptonshire bounced back to secure a four-wicket victory in a final afternoon run chase. Confidence restored!

The final match of 1989 was against Warwickshire at Edgbaston, the Northampton humiliation still very much in mind.

Edgbaston looked particular drab and dreary in the end-of-summer rain. I like the ground a lot, it holds many happy memories, but, like most vast Test arenas in the wet with a handful of spectators huddling under umbrellas, there were other places I'd much rather have been.

In all two days were washed out but at least the damp squib enabled me to catch up with Edgbaston press doyen Mike Beddow and his sidekick JJ.

The latter's lunchtime tipple was famously dubbed a Mickey Mouse – half a pint of lager added to half a pint of bitter in case you were wondering!

Northamptonshire finished fifth in the Championship table, a promising initial return on their large investment, but the one-day campaign was nothing to write home about. **115**

Ambrose enjoyed solid enough bowling figures in his first year with the club but in some quarters – among media and supporters – there was a suggestion that he should be doing more.

Felton spoke up for Ambrose, who he believed found it hard adapting to life in England.

He said: "It was hard on Curtly who struggled to shake off his doubters in his first few seasons.

"A crisis meeting called by Lamby brought things to a head and Curtly himself helped lift all the tension.

"Lamby had given us all a bit of a rollicking and was questioning the enthusiasm of his bowlers.

"Curtly, who had his feet up on the table in the dressing room, suddenly announced that he had something to say.

"He said that bowling was very hard work and that if anyone asked him if he wanted to bowl then he would say no. However, if anyone told him to bowl, then he would bowl!

"Again, it must have been hard for Curtly adapting to the culture of English county cricket.

"His father had died before he came out and he had his partner Bridget and a little girl to look after. It wasn't easy for him.

"Nowadays he is playing bass guitar in a band in Antigua and is loving life. When we see him over here, he has his guitar with him!

Ripley said: "It was effectively between Curtly and Winston for a place in the side in Curtly's early years at the club.

"Curtly was a completely different bowler from Winston. He would bowl either a short or a full length at good pace.

"I didn't warm to Curtly at first. He was playing more than Winston and there was considerable feeling that Winnie, who was well liked and who had contributed a lot, was hard done by.

"Curtly was very much his own person but as time went on he gradually integrated himself into the set up and became good value in the dressing room.

"He got more involved in team discussions and it was always very interesting to see when he got annoyed out on the field.

"He obviously didn't bowl flat out all the time playing for us but when something had got to him you could see his knees really getting up as he ran in.

"The ball would really come in but it didn't matter how fast he bowled, he would always retain control.

"Capes had a big part to play in bringing Curtly in to the fold. He was very good to him, especially when we were away from home.

"They would usually travel together, and for some of the journey Curtly would usually be munching on a chocolate bar and getting crumbs everywhere over the car's upholstery. Capes was pretty tolerant of that!"

Coverdale felt that captain Lamb's man management skills, in respect of the two West Indian overseas players, left something to be desired.

He said: "We had scouted Ambrose back in 1987, on the recommendation of agent Jack Simmons, the former Lancashire player.

"Ambrose was playing for Haslingden in the Lancashire League and Brian Reynolds and I went up to have a look at him the week before the NatWest final.

"What we saw was a tall, gangling lad with very short trousers! He could certainly bowl with pace and accuracy and also fielded in the slips.

"Whenever he took a wicket he celebrated as if he had just scored the winning goal in a Cup final.

"Our overseas players at the time were Roger Harper and Winston Davis but we thought that both of them would be touring with the West Indies in 1988.     **117**

"Accordingly we decided to take a gamble on this very raw 'unknown' having brought him down to Northampton to practise just before the end of the 1987 season.

"We planned to have another more experienced bowler as our main overseas player for 1988. However within months Curtly had taken the record number of wickets in one season in the Red Stripe Cup and been catapulted into the West Indies side, ironically replacing Winston.

"So we had to wait until 1989 before he arrived at Northampton, Dennis Lillee's comeback filling the overseas gap in 1988.

"In my opinion Lamby initially didn't show himself to be a great man manager with Curtly and Winston. Once Curtly had arrived it was clear that Lamby saw him as his number one choice and naturally Winston did not take that well, justifiably as Lamby was being unfair to a very fine bowler in his own right who was very popular in the team.

"Curtly was naïve and inexperienced on his introduction to county cricket, and to domestic life generally. On three occasions he got to the ground and discovered that he had locked himself out of his house!

"He was already one of the world's leading bowlers but the expectation that he could deliver a consistently high standard in county cricket was very unfair. Too much was expected of him."


## ENGLAND FOUR – AND AMBROSE IS FIVE!

Ambrose found himself in opposition with four of his county colleagues in early 1990 when Allan Lamb, Wayne Larkins, Rob Bailey and David Capel were all selected for the England tour of the West Indies.

Capel takes up the story of an enthralling three months with England in the Caribbean. **118**

He said: "It was an interesting series as the West Indies were expected to do well against an England team including some inexperienced players, among them Nasser Hussain, Angus Fraser and Devon Malcolm.

"We had four representatives and Curtly Ambrose was playing for the West Indies, whose party also included Eldine Baptiste who was to join our staff in 1991.

"To have four Northamptonshire players in an England eleven must have been a very proud moment for the likes of Lynn Wilson and all those others who had invested heavily in the county cricket club. It hadn't happened before and it hasn't happened since.

"Before we went out, we had a few conditioning sessions with Geoff Boycott and we were as well prepared as any Test team going out to play a series in the Caribbean.

"When we got out there, we felt the scenarios were more intense than the actual reality but it was a very useful preparation phase for those with no experience of a West Indies tour.

"We recorded a memorable win in the First Test at Jamaica's Sabina Park. The victory certainly raised a few eyebrows around the world.

"Even Prime Minister Margaret Thatcher sent a message of congratulations so we felt a real sense of national pride in our achievement!

"Bowling straight after lunch on the first day, I had Richie Richardson caught by Gladstone Small off a mistimed pull, a big wicket, and also dismissed Carlisle Best who was caught behind.

"Gordon Greenidge was run out by a yard by Devon Malcolm and he then bowled Viv Richards who was on fire!

"When we batted, Lamby scored a great 132 to give us a useful first innings lead. The pitch was medium paced and captain Graham Gooch's bowling strategy was good, telling us to bowl just short of a length on the offside. **119**

"We stayed disciplined and with pretty much a relatively inexperienced bowling attack – Devon Malcolm, Angus Fraser (who took 5-18), Gladstone Small and me – we bowled them out twice!

"We didn't have many to get in the second innings and Wayne Larkins scored the winning run in a nine-wicket victory!"

Gooch recalled: "The media had us down for a blackwash but by the end of this tour we had made people stand up and realise that we had a team to be taken seriously again.

"In the victory at Sabina Park, David Capel had picked up the wickets of Richardson and Best in a tremendous first innings bowling display by the whole attack.

"Allan Lamb came up with a brilliant century when we batted to give us a good lead.

"And on the final day, we knocked off the last two West Indies second innings wickets and, with 40 needed to win, I got myself out but Wayne Larkins hit the runs to give us victory.

"The win was a great thrill for me, to beat the West Indies on their own patch.

"It was the first time an England side had done this in 16 years and this against the best team in the world!

"It was an unforgettable memory for everyone out there, either playing or supporting the England team."

The Second Test in Georgetown, Guyana, was completely washed out by rain and England went into the Third Test, at Port of Spain, Trinidad coveting a 1-0 series lead.

Capel said: "This match was the turning point of the series, without a doubt.

"We had lost skipper Graham Gooch with a broken hand and also pace bowler Angus Fraser.

They were both key players, Fraser eventually being replaced by Phillip DeFreitas. **120**

"I felt I batted well in the first innings, shepherding through the tail to ensure we got an extra 80-100 towards the end.

"We were again very competitive and got ourselves in a great position before the rain arrived in the second innings, allowing the pitch to sweat under plastic sheeting.

"Gooch went retired hurt but, needing 70 runs to win, the West Indies employed tactics to slow the game right down – we thought we might get 30 or so overs, in the end we got fewer than 20.

"The West Indies, in the knowledge that on a gloomy day it would be dark by 5pm, decided to bowl very few overs an hour and they were allowed to do so unchecked.

"There is no twilight in the Caribbean, it goes from light to dark very rapidly.

"They came up with long run-ups, false starts, sawdust delays and continual Desmond Haynes field changes – they were in danger of going two down and this was a master class in saving a Test.

"Their bowlers were also bowling quite a few bouncer per over, so there were only a couple of balls in any over that you could actually hit.

"I was batting with Jack Russell. With 30 runs needed to win it said 10 overs to go on the board and it became evident that we weren't going to get the runs.

"We got into the dressing room and five minutes later it was completely dark.

"We felt like we had been deprived of victory and perhaps psychologically the West Indies came away feeling they had achieved."

And so to the cauldron of Bridgetown, Barbados for the Fourth Test where the West Indies, still trailing in the series, knew they really had to turn up the heat.

Capel added: "Lamby was captain for this game with Gooch out injured and I bowled pretty well for 3-88 in their first knock.

"In Bridgetown the weather was hot, the pitch was flat and there was no swing – it was hard work. It was all about line, length and control.

"Haynes hit a good century in the second innings but we were also missing Fraser who had previously forged a good partnership with Malcolm.

"We were up against it in our final innings. We hadn't had a great start, Ned had gone for a duck and Rob Bailey was out controversially.

"But Jack Russell, in as night watchman, batted for most of the last day with Robin Smith.

"It was a war of attrition, up until the time Ambrose got to grips with the second new ball.

"He got Russell out, the crowd got behind their team and the pitch seemed to behave differently.

"Ambrose's knees started to get up under his chin and he got a lot of lbw decisions with the ball staying low.

"Ambrose ended up with eight wickets and was chaired off the field at the end.

"I can remember the passion of the crowd that final afternoon.

"It was a cauldron, the locals were on their feet and the large numbers of England fans were eventually subdued."

Bailey found himself the centre of media attention during the Barbados test, the victim of a controversial dismissal that helped turn the tide of the West Indies.

He said: "It was a great honour for me and Capes to join Ned and Lamby in the England squad.

"Everyone thought we were going to be wiped out but we won the first Test in Jamaica and I remember the fantastic party that followed that night.

"The Second Test was washed out so if we'd won in Trinidad in the Third Test we'd have guaranteed ourselves at least a share of the series.

"Capes would have contributed to that victory had the elements and some clear sportsmanship not intervened. **122**

"Malcolm had bowled well and Capes was looking good with the bat.

"The West Indies were up against it and they did everything they could to avoid defeat.

"The fact that they managed to do so took the psychological momentum back towards the West Indies as we prepared for the Fourth Test on a good track in Barbados.

"A lot of England fans had come out for the last two Tests, which were virtually back to back.

"I won't forget the match in a hurry. Lamby put the West Indies in and they built up a big first innings total, and I got 17 in the first dig which ended up with us being behind.

"Richards remained under pressure to win the match and satisfy the locals who more and more were beginning to get on his back.

"He set us a pretty big fourth-innings total to win the match and little over a day to get the runs or, more likely from our point of view, save the game.

"With the light closing in on day four, Larkins went for a duck which meant that he picked up a pair in the Test.

"I joined Alec Stewart and had got to six runs out of a total of ten facing up to my county team-mate Ambrose.

"I pushed forward to Ambrose and the ball carried through to wicketkeeper Jeff Dujon but went nowhere near the bat.

"There was no appeal from Ambrose but all of a sudden I became aware of Viv dancing down the field claiming a caught behind.

"The next minute, umpire Lloyd Barker had raised his finger and I was walking back to the pavilion.

"I took a chunk out of the dressing room fridge in my frustration. Gladstone Small then went in as night-watchman but he too was dismissed so we closed the day on 15-3.

"I wasn't much in the mood for talking that night and there was a lot of criticism being aimed at Richards and Barker. **123**

"Commentator Chris Martin-Jenkins said in his report: 'If that was gamesmanship or professionalism, I'm not sure what cheating is'.

"This developed into a row which was the talk of the island and Martin-Jenkins was taken off the local radio station and treated as a pariah.

"Some years later I caught up with his son Robin who, unbeknown to me, had been out in the West Indies with his dad watching that series.

"Robin said that life was made very uncomfortable for them and it was an experience he wasn't likely to forget in a hurry.

"Both Richards and Ambrose were pretty laid back about it, you know 'that's life, these things happen'.

"I am pretty philosophical about it but in truth that sort of approach to winning a game of cricket remains alien to me.

"In spite of some heroics from Russell and Smith, Ambrose eventually ran through us at the close of the final day and the West Indies had levelled the series.

"We didn't put up much of a fight during the final Test in Antigua, which started just a few days after the one in Barbados had finished.

"The momentum had swung back to the West Indies and we were all physically and emotionally drained.

"We returned back to England, defeated but proud of what we'd achieved. It was a great experience and one I will never forget!"

At scores level, the Fifth Test in Antigua was a game too far for the England cricketers.

Capel said: "It had been a long tour in terms of intensity, we only had one day off between the Barbados and Antigua Tests which were put together to accommodate the tourist interest.

"We were on a bit of a downer after Barbados and again it was very hot.

John Capel kept a scrapbook of son David's cricketing career and here we pick out a few landmarks along the way....

1977
Northamptonshire Schools Under-15s

The County under-15 team line-up for the camera. Back row, left to right, David Capel, David Heathfield, Alan Harlow, Roger Ball, Kevin Hawkes, Roger Flowers, Nigel Oldan, Peter Unsworth. Front row, Jimby Wake (manager), William Kellaher, Nicky Stairs, John Ebsworth (capt), Simon Banks, Andy Penford, Steve Ellis (assistant manager).

1979
Learning a trade – as a cobbler of course!

David Capel: Big chance. Picture: John Seamark

# 1981
## Northamptonshire v Sri Lanka – first-class debut

# 1986
## Century v Leicestershire at the County Ground

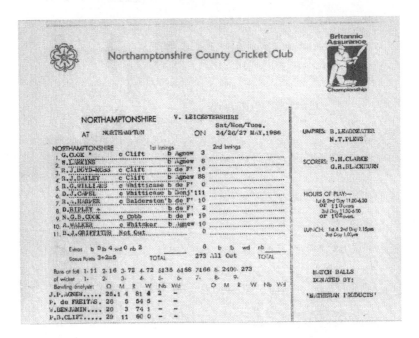

## Headlines on Test debut at Headingley

# Calm Capel lifts gloom

### HENRY BLOFELD

THERE ARE few things more exciting in sport than to see a young and talented player establish himself at international level. On a day of almost unrelieved gloom for England, David Capel's innings of 53 told not only of his ability but also of an unusual maturity.

It is not often that a newcomer gives such a strong impression of calmness as well as capability in a crisis. Naturally, he was nervous when he first went in, but at 31 for 5 he will have taken some heart from the fact that he could hardly do worse than some of his more illustrious colleagues who had gone before him.

It took him 13 balls to get off the mark and he controlled his nerves admirably during this difficult time. Ian Botham was at the other end and several times stopped in mid-wicket to have a few words with Capel and to encourage him which will have been a great help. His 14th ball produced a single to fine leg off Imran Khan and after that Capel batted with surprising assurance. He is an old-fashioned cricketer in that he stands at the crease with his bat on the ground facing his right toe cap and he is also, out-

wardly at any rate, an unemotional and undemonstrative cricketer.

Just before lunch he played a lovely straight drive for four off Mudassar Nazar which should have helped his appetite. The pitch was awkward and every run had to be chiselled out of it and Capel simply went on always playing straight, treating every ball on its merits and he never looked in serious trouble. His excellent temperament was again revealed as he approached his 50, which he reached with a handsome drive for four off Mohsin Kamal. It was a most impressive and auspicious first Test innings.

THE INDEPENDENT FRIDAY 3RD JULY, 1987

### THE THIRD TEST

# Hero at high noon

NEW BOY David Capel spared England from acute embarrassment after a blunder by captain Mike Gatting yesterday on the opening day of the third Cornhill Test at Headingley.

The blond 24-year-old from Northants marked his England debut with a defiant 53, while his colleagues stumbled to 136 all out.

But there was a major question mark over whether England, on winning the toss, should have batted first, given Headingley's reputation as a batsman's graveyard.

Leeds groundsman Keith Boyce announced in advance of the game that the Test

## Capel to the rescue as Gatting blunders

### GRAHAM OTWAY reports from Headingley

wicket, newly laid in 1984 and in use for the first time was "all his own baby."

But it quickly became clear he had been unable to eradicate some of the mischievous genetic traits of its predecessors.

With inconsistent bounce and patchy overhead cloud making the odd ball swing as well as seam, England struggled from the moment Imran Khan's third ball nipped back to trap Tim Robinson lbw.

#### Valuable

Gatting's decision to bat first made a mockery of including Capel, a bowler capable of exploiting those traditional first-day conditions, and omitting John Emburey, the extra spinner, who might have been invaluable if England survive long enough to bowl in the fourth innings.

But at least, batting at seven, Capel was able to shore up England's fragile order. When he shuffled nervously out to the wicket, England looked shattered at 31 for five.

It was exactly 12 o'clock the perfect scene for a high-noon showdown between some of the world's leading all-

rounders. Pakistan's two players — the veteran Imran Khan and his protege Wasim Akram — were steaming in at full tilt. Waiting for the Northants youngster was Ian Botham.

Botham played responsibly for a shade under two hours, making 26, with only two boundaries.

But old habits die hard. Having had one fearsome drive against Mudassar stopped in the covers, he could not resist chasing after a wide one two balls later — and was caught behind.

Taking 20 minutes to score his first Test run, Capel played and missed regularly. But that, at least, was more impressive than the efforts of the more senior David Gower, Mike Gatting and Jack Richards, who all fell to grave errors of misjudgement — and out without offering a shot.

When Pakistan began their reply in the last 90 minutes of the day, Foster accounted for Shoaib Mohammad and Mudassar Nazar, but then had both Mansoor Akhtar and Salim Yousuf dropped at slip by Phil Edmonds and substitute Emburey respectively.

DAVID CAPEL . . . runs

England
First Innings

| | |
|---|---|
| B C Broad c Salim Yousuf b Akram | 8 |
| R T Robinson lbw Imran | 0 |
| C W J Athey c Salim Yousuf b Imran | 8 |
| D I Gower b Imran | 10 |
| *M W Gatting lbw Akram | 8 |
| I T Botham c Salim Yousuf b Mudassar | 26 |
| D J Capel c and b Mohsin Kamal | 53 |
| †C J Richards lbw Akram | 0 |
| N G Foster c Malik b Mohsin Kamal | 9 |
| P H Edmonds c Salim Yousuf b M Kamal | 0 |
| G R Dilley not out | 1 |
| Extras (b 1, lb 6, w 1, nb 1) | 11 |
| Total | 136 |

Fall of wickets: 1-1, 2-13, 3-13, 4-31, 5-31, 6-95, 7-112, 8-133, 9-133.
Bowling: Imran Khan 19-3-37-3; Wasim Akram 14-4-36-3; Abdul Qadir 6-0-14-0; Mudassar Nazar 14-5-10-1; Mohsin Kamal 8-4-2-22-3.

Pakistan
First Innings

| | |
|---|---|
| Mudassar Nazar lbw Foster | 24 |
| Shoaib Mohammad c Richards b Foster | 16 |
| Mansoor Akhtar not out | 24 |
| †Salim Yousuf not out | 8 |
| Extras (lb 7, nb 1) | 8 |
| Total (2 wkts) | 76 |

Fall of wickets: 1-22, 2-60.
Bowling: Dilley 5-1-13-0; Foster 10-3-27-2; Capel 6-1-14-0; Edmonds 4-1-13-0.

1987
England v Pakistan – Test debut at Headlingley

1987
Pakistan v England – 98 in Karachi, highest Test score

## 1989
## Two centuries in match against Sussex at Hove

**Two centuries in a match for Northants all-rounder**

# Stunning Capel boosts Test claim

14-6-89

by Andy Roberts

## 1990
## Four Northamptonshire players named on England tour

**England Tour to West Indies January to April 1990**

| | |
|---|---|
| Captain: | G.A. Gooch (Essex) |
| Vice Captain: | A.J. Lamb (Northamptonshire) |
| | R.J. Bailey (Northamptonshire) |
| | D.J. Capel (Northamptonshire) |
| | P.A.J. DeFreitas (Lancashire) |
| | R.M. Ellcock (Middlesex) |
| | A.R.C. Fraser (Middlesex) |
| | E.E. Hemmings (Nottinghamshire) |
| | N. Hussain (Essex) |
| | W. Larkins (Northamptonshire) |
| | D.E. Malcolm (Derbyshire) |
| | K.T. Medlycott (Surrey) |
| | R.C. Russell (Gloucestershire) |
| | G.C. Small (Warwickshire) |
| | R.A. Smith (Hampshire) |
| | A.J. Stewart (Surrey) |
| Manager: | P.M. Lush |
| Team Manager: | M.J. Stewart |
| Physiotherapist: | L.G. Brown |
| Scorer: | S.P. Austin |

1990
Ollie's Boys on tour in the West Indies!

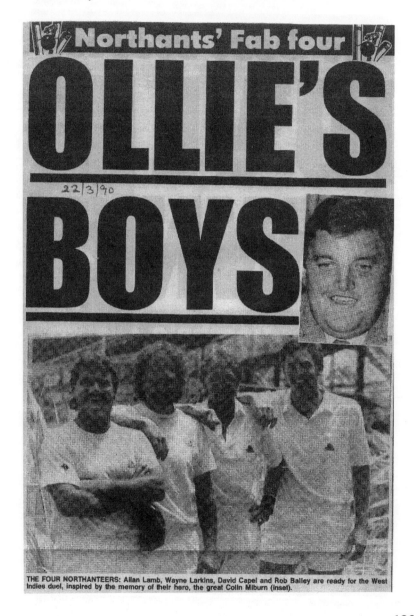

Northants' Fab four

OLLIE'S

22/3/90

BOYS

THE FOUR NORTHANTEERS: Allan Lamb, Wayne Larkins, David Capel and Rob Bailey are ready for the West Indies duel, inspired by the memory of their hero, the great Colin Milburn (inset).

1990
Telegram from the Prime Minister

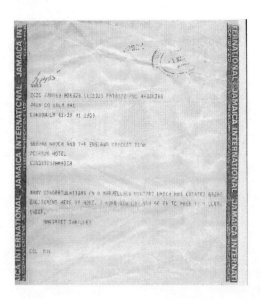

1992
NatWest Trophy winners v Leicestershire – at last!

CUP JOY ENDS
FINAL GLOOM

1998
End of the road as a player... badly done

**TALKING SPORT**
**By Andy Roberts**

NORTHANTS cricket is in a shambolic state, on and off the field. But its decision makers really plumbed the depths with the premature sacking of long-serving David Capel.

A press conference yesterday raised hopes that, at long last, Northants were prepared to take some constructive action upon the state of terminal decline which has been seeping into Wantage Road for some considerable time.

But the conference made no mention of streamlining, rooting out under-achievers or changing direction.

Instead, it signalled the end of the road for a cricketer who has barely featured in the first team picture for the last couple of seasons.

A cricketer who has been the Tudor Rose 'heart and soul' in a 19-year career blessed with many ups and blighted with many downs, personal as well as professional. A cricketer who, frankly, deserved much better.

Capel has become a shameful and quite unnecessary sacrifice on the altar of political expediency. From what has been made public, there can be no other explanation.

"The pitch was fast and true and this was a routine victory to take the series. I went for a hundred and there was no coming back after they got you in their sights."

West Indies 2 England 1, final score - the outing in Antigua was to prove Capel's last international appearance for England.

His former county skipper Cook said: "His record stands up to his credit. It might not be earth shattering but he certainly didn't disgrace himself in this respect.

"He didn't play that often for England, but if you analyse the games he did play you will see he contributed some significant performances for the national team and stood up well to Pakistan in 1987 in particular.

"And for Northamptonshire, his abilities gave the side a lot of balance, which is what was required.

"I think David realised that as a batsman he might struggle to get into the side on a regular basis.

"He saw the opportunity to add another string to his bow as a bowler and his sheer ambition saw him through to his goal.

"He would have benefited even more if the selection policy had not been so much of a revolving door, at least this policy is a lot more consistent today.

"So many cricketers, Capel included, suffered from the 'in and out' policy of the time.

"If you are given a good run in the national side you feel more reassured and the pressure to perform and succeed is alleviated.

"David put a lot of pressure on himself quite apart from that which then applied in the England arena and the uncertainty over his international prospects would not have helped him.

"His body withstanding, his desire to get the best out of himself was admirable.

"If there was ever anyone out there wanting 'to be the best that you can be' then that was David Capel." **133**

Back on the domestic front, Northamptonshire unveiled a new pairing to rival Cook and Larkins at the top of the order – Alan Fordham and Nigel Felton, the F-Plan!

The 1990 home campaign got underway at Cambridge University at Fenners, a match I missed as I shook off the jet lag from my Caribbean trip following the Northamptonshire boys.

The season got underway properly with a Sunday match at Leicester but the programming was tough on the Test players who were not long back from their gruelling schedule.

The first Championship action came at Yorkshire with the team camped in a hotel at Brighouse, a few miles outside of Leeds.

The whole team found themselves out of the hotel during the early hours of day two, courtesy of a fire alarm.

But the drama did little to unsettle the county batsmen as Lamb and Fordham made hay in the Headingley sunshine. So much for A Block!

Lamb scored 235 and Fordham 206 as the pair celebrated a then club record stand of 393 en route to a first-innings declaration of 498-3 – 300 ahead of the Tykes.

The home side were dismissed for 250 on the final day and Northamptonshire were off to a flying start in all competitions, having already chalked up Benson and Hedges Cup and Sunday wins.

Some good times were spent in Brian's fish bar and the Three Horseshoes pub, favourite stop-offs for the cricketing fraternity in Leeds.

The Headingley trip represented a brief watershed in relations between the media and Windies star Ambrose, who has never been keen to talk to the press.

Here, however, the local boys wanted a view on the West Indies tour, not least the controversial Bailey dismissal, which to that point had been swerved.

Ambrose was press-ganged into giving an interview by the club and it made for an interesting change. **134**

But on Bailey's situation he simply shrugged his shoulders and said: "That's cricket, sometime it goes for you and other times it doesn't. We all make mistakes."

## OFF BEAM IN A MISERABLE MAY

It didn't take long for the wheels to start coming off the wagon and May 3 brought the first rattle.

Derbyshire were the first Championship visitors and injuries to Lamb, Nick Cook and then Ripley resulted in Northamptonshire losing within two days, dismissed in the second innings for 50 although they were three batsmen short.

The match was written off as 'one of those games' but going into the remainder of the Benson & Hedges Cup group matches, the early gloss was beginning to fade.

The Essex game in the Benson & Hedges Cup featured a number of Windies tour reunions but Northamptonshire, under the stewardship of Larkins, were not at their best.

The off-spinner Jimmy Govan was given a rare outing but was given just one over by Larkins, whose handling of the attack was far from imaginative.

The supporters demanded a clear improvement for the next game, at home to Scotland, but things were about to get a whole lot worse.

Govan this time got 11 overs against his compatriots but 95 from Scots skipper Iain Philip steered his side to an improbable 231-8 and the county finished two runs short in spite of a century from skipper Larkins.

Lamb was in the press box, purring over Ambrose's ability while at the same time seeking a publicity opportunity around getting a cheap bed for his son.

And somewhere over in Corby, a lone piper was delivering a lament to Northamptonshire cricket...

The slump needed to be halted and there was opportunity to do so quickly in Nottingham.                **135**

But Capel had injured his kneecap during a nets session with Walker and both he and Larkins also joined the growing injury list, which promoted Bailey as the team's latest captain.

The side were defeated by three wickets but put in a much better fighting performance which brought some encouragement.

Bailey kept the captaincy for the home match with Warwickshire which had a habit of being eventful.

This meeting was no exception as the second day of what had been an evenly-fought contest exploded in controversy.

With the visitors gradually turning the screw and building a big first-innings score, Northamptonshire's pace trio of Thomas, Robinson and Ambrose came into the firing line from the umpires.

Robinson was withdrawn from the attack, Thomas was warned and then Ambrose ended up being disciplined by the club for starting a 'beamer war' with Warwickshire's abrasive Dermot Reeve, who went on to score an unbeaten 202.

It was hard on Bailey, finding himself in the middle of another Ambrose row just six weeks after the Bridgetown barney.

Capel had returned to action in another Championship defeat to Nottinghamshire at Trent Bridge in what had turned out to a miserable month of May.

Ripley said: "Was David Capel a selfish player? There were some certainly who would have that view of him.

"But I wasn't one of them and in that respect I think he was much misunderstood.

"The thing with David was that he was sure he could influence the match and felt he should be given the chance to do so.

"Some would raise eyebrows when he went on about batting higher up the order or wanting to bowl with the wind.

"But he had so much passion for the club. He wanted to win and he was determined that he could play a part in achieving the victory. **136**

"My abiding memory of him was this match at Trent Bridge where he played through a knee injury.

"As a bowler, Capes liked to attack and wasn't afraid to dig it in short and show some aggression.

"I would describe him as a thinking bowler but he maybe thought about it too much, to the extent that he was over-analytical.

"When he was caught up in the emotion of a game, particularly when someone had got after him, you could see the kettle brewing and you knew he would soon be steaming in.

"This was the way he played. Like the cracked knee game, it would be like an outpouring, something he needed to get out of his system.

Coverdale said: "For me, we had assembled our strongest-ever squad in the summer of 1990.

"This was evidenced by the Caribbean tour at the start of the year when we had David Capel, Rob Bailey, Allan Lamb and Wayne Larkins playing for England and Curtly Ambrose for the West Indies.

"If you add the likes of Greg Thomas, Nick Cook and Richard Williams to the mix, we had great strength in all areas.

"We got off to a brilliant start, beating Yorkshire by an innings and plenty in our first match but then everything went disastrously wrong.

"We somehow managed to lose every game we played in the month of May, which took some doing, during which time we also got through four captains.

"We finished a match against Derbyshire with only seven fit players from the eleven who had started the game, and suffered an ignominious defeat to Scotland in the Benson and Hedges Cup.

"We then had the 'beamer wars' game against Warwickshire when Rob Bailey was in charge of the side, I think it was his first Championship match as captain.     **137**

"Dermot Reeve antagonised Curtly Ambrose who bowled him a few at head height.

"To compound matters, the two umpires in the middle – Don Oslear and Barry Dudleston – clearly didn't get on at the time.

"After a series of meetings over two days Ambrose had to make a much-publicised apology to Reeve.

"Grudgingly, I would add, but we had more problems in the shape of Oslear who reported us to Lord's for poor behaviour and claimed that Greg Thomas had sworn at him during the game.

"Months and months later, another Welshman – not a fast bowler - confessed to me that he may have made an indiscreet remark towards Oslear!"

Capel and Ambrose were in good form on the opening day of the Warwickshire return, the home side dismissed for 202.

Northamptonshire posted 318-8 declared and their hosts were helped by a rain delay on the final day, creeping to 142-9 and match drawn.

The county were at the Cobden Hotel in Birmingham – virtually opposite the Strathallan – and Capel was in a relaxed groove.

Over a drink, he said: "I'm a great believer in the saying, 'if you do well, you should celebrate success.'

"Wind down and spend some quality time with your mates.

"Equally, if you haven't done so well then find the guys who have had a good day, rather than sitting in a room going into a spin."

Capel's relaxed frame of mind continued into the home games against Glamorgan at the start of June, with a hundred in the Sunday fixture in front of the Sky TV cameras.

Northamptonshire won an entertaining clash by ten runs, a long-overdue victory – the first since the one at Headingley on 26 April!

Capel admitted to extra-special motivation – the television profile and a certain IVA Richards in the Glamorgan side!

Capel said: "I did raise my game when Viv Richards was around. He was my hero and I wanted to impress him. The same can also be said when the cameras were in town and Tony Greig and Geoff Boycott were on the ground. For me, they were all icons of the game and I naturally wanted to deliver."

In the three-day game, Thomas took 7-75 against his old mates but Glamorgan – set 307 for victory on the final afternoon - got home with six wickets to spare thanks to a century from Sir Viv!

Geoff Cook chose a break from the cricket to announce his retirement with a managerial move back home to Durham beckoning in preparation for the county's elevation to the first-class county list.

With news breaking of another icon of the game receiving a knighthood, the county scorecard included a first on the Kiwis side – an entry for Sir Richard Hadlee.

But Sir Richard actually sat out the match. The scorecard became a collector's item nevertheless!

In this 'white wicket' year, where runs were aplenty up and down the country, Capel's soaring form continued to build.

He hit 123 out of Northamptonshire's first innings 279-9 declared against the tourists and followed that up with a second innings unbeaten 65 in a rain-affected draw.

Sir Richard Hadlee said: "I had been given the match off and arrived in Northampton on the second day of the game at Wantage Road.

"As I walked into the dressing room, the lads formed a line and bowed and Martin Snedden then proceeded to dub me with his cricket bat!

"The match was also significant for another reason – David Capel scored a century against us. **139**

"To score a hundred against a touring team is an important and special moment in your career because it is an international match and can mean so much more than other games."

Capel was enjoying himself out in the middle and, in the murk of the final day, actually ordered the lights in the press box to be temporarily turned off as they were proving a distraction!

So for a few minutes, deadlines were put on hold as the journos, incredibly patiently, obeyed the edict from the middle!


## DUNSTABLE'S HARRY STOTTLE!

Back on Championship duties at Wardown Park, Northamptonshire registered yet another defeat against Middlesex.

Luton brought the scholarly late Richard 'Dick' Streeton of The Times into the fold.

Quite appropriate really, as much of his visit was concentrated on his relationship with his wife Mavis and the merits of Origami!

A lovely man, Streeton was hard of hearing but loved the press box banter, and there was plenty of that around in this particular match.

The press box fun extended warmly across Wardown Park with the help of public information announcer Ramshackle Ron who also travelled from the County Ground to the other 'home' matches.

Encouraged by the club's irascible commercial manager Graham Alsop, Ron was encouraged to read out some public information announcements during the course of the final day's play.

The first was for a missing child 'Mahatma Coat' to report to the pavilion attendant. **140**

And as the ripples of laughter spread across the ground – and with Ron blissfully unaware of the merriment he was creating – the announcements followed thick and fast with players and journalists all getting in on the act.

I cannot recall them all but do remember a call for a Mr 'IP Freely' to call home and I think 'Hugh Jarse' was also summoned...

There was definitely a call a call for 'Archie Medes' of the Houghton Regis Water Company to telephone his office because of a leak.

And it was only a matter of time before 'Harry Stottle' of the Greek Taverna in Dunstable was directed to the Wardown Park office to pick up a message.

All delivered in Ron's trademark burr!... the final missive was reserved for the good sponsors of the NatWest Bank, present and correct and many of them well-oiled in their hospitality tents.

'Would a Mr Robin Banks, from our sponsors NatWest, please contact Bedfordshire Police...'

Cue loud guffaws from the banking fraternity and enough off-the-field mirth to offset the latest depressing loss on the club's results spreadsheet.

The county batsmen scored in huge chunks to post 360-2 on the board against minnows Staffordshire in the NatWest Trophy.

A left-arm paceman for the visitors, by the name of Paul Taylor, conceded 92 runs off his 12 overs.

This statistic was to become strangely significant in the fullness of time!

One of Nigel Felton's highlights was his return to Taunton at the end of June and posting a century against the club that had let him go.

He said: "That was a great feeling, even if Capes famously declared afterwards that his grandmother could have scored a century on that pitch! To be fair it was pretty flat!
**141**

"I didn't agree with him on that but I could relate to the frustration that he must have often have felt when he would see lesser batsmen than him going in higher up the order and scoring runs.

"I have no doubt that if he had concentrated on just his batting he would have been a player of the highest quality.

"He had a good technique and very good balance at the crease, which set him in good stead.

"I know he also got frustrated by the fact that bowling was hard work and he often felt that it was getting in the way of his batting.

"He will always question whether or not he should have concentrated on his batting rather than on being an all-rounder.

"I would put it as simply as this – yes, the all-rounder role took a lot out of him.

"But how fortunate to be in the position to have an abundance of talent to perform both as a batsman and as a bowler to a very high standard.

"Capes was a match winner, with both bat and ball, and as such was an invaluable player within the team.

"He would get you the big wicket and had the very happy knack of getting good players out."

I wasn't driving for the Sunday match at Tring and arrived at the ground a good two hours before the start, a quick drink at the bar before the match turning into two then three or four.

This was owing to the fact that Searby was also in tow with the Yorkshire Mafia.

And it was an hour or so into the Yorkshire innings before we finally took our seats in the press 'trailer' a little the worse for wear.

The trailer was old, rustic and dusty, much to Searby's bemusement and increasing annoyance.

The annoyance turned to belligerence when a rusty old nail tore into the cloth of his favourite navy blazer.   **142**

Spotting Coverdale, who had popped along to the customary picnic, in the vicinity, Searby then proceeded to track him around the boundary rope, waving his blazer in the air and demanding the club recompense him for laundry and repair!

The proceedings ended with a Yorkshire victory, yours truly almost getting involved in a bar room brawl while watching the World Cup Final between Germany and Argentina and one of my travelling companions, who had a gallon of ale on board, mistaking a hedge for the front passenger seat of his chariot back to Northampton!

The defeat had concentrated minds, not only among disgruntled supporters – who demanded an open meeting with captain Lamb at Wantage Road - but in the club committee room as well.

Coverdale said: "The wheels were off and everyone at the club was at a very low ebb.

"So much so that Frank Chamberlain, the then club President and chairman of the Test and County Cricket Board, felt drastic action might be needed.

"Frank was always very good to me and very supportive as my first chairman at Northamptonshire.

"I could set my watch by the 8.20am morning phone call that arrived precisely on time every morning when, for no more than five minutes, we would discuss the business of the day.

"The night before our second round NatWest tie at home to Nottinghamshire, Frank hosted a garden party at his home in east Northamptonshire.

"During what was a very convivial evening he took me to one side and he made it clear that if we went out of the NatWest to Nottinghamshire – our season effectively over – then it would have to be the end of the road for the captain Allan Lamb.

"As it turned out, we went on to beat Nottinghamshire. And the rest, as they say, is history."          **143**

A blazing hot day saw Lamb win the toss and activate his battle plan – bat first and bat the opposition into submission!

The county did just that, scoring 274-6 from their 60 overs - a winning total but, come the end of a long day, only by 24 runs.

Capel was in brilliant form, taking the Notts attack apart with a smattering of towering sixes which pinged merrily off the top of the packed sponsor tents at the football end of the ground.

Rob Bailey's off-spin then tied the visitors down and a quarter-final place was booked.

Now ten years without a major trophy in the cabinet, the pressure was on this talented side to succeed.

The white wickets and hot weather was paving the way for some massive scores but some pretty tedious cricketing contests in the Championship.

But on the NatWest front the county were now positively buzzing and a feelgood vibe was beginning to return to the side.

The county were asked to bat first in their home quarter-final and it was never going to be straightforward against a formidable Worcestershire side.

The county totalled 263 on a blazing hot day in front of a packed house at Wantage Road.

Worcestershire fell four runs short on 259-9 with Botham taking the man-of-the-match award in defeat.

Mark Robinson's 3-33 from 12 overs for the county, silencing all of Worcestershire's big guns, may have been more deserving.

Felton said: "I got some opportunities this year. Forders, who I had got to know quite well, changed virtually overnight and really began to establish himself as an all-out attacking batsman.

"He was a very cautious guy off the field but on it he began to play as if he hadn't got a care in the world.    **144**

"We ended up opening together and kept scoring runs, to the point that the group meetings held between Lamby, Wayne Larkins and Nick Cook – the Politburo – agreed that I had earned my place in the line-up.

"This was the year where they changed the pitches in favour of the batsmen and altered the seam on the ball, again in favour of the batsmen.

"As a result, I scored a lot of runs and really began to enjoy myself in the middle.

"Watching Forders in full flow was a treat and he helped himself to a lot of runs.

"In one game against Worcestershire, he scored five fours off Neal Radford in quick time and none of them were bad balls!

"And Capes too couldn't do anything wrong with the bat. I think he was struggling with his back at the time so he was probably in a lot of discomfort.

"The rest of us probably didn't appreciate his struggle at the time. Capes could be a little needy and some of the lads felt it was too much.

"He must have found it hard and his sheer determination got him through."

The heat was well and truly on with the mercury peaking at 99F on day one of the Championship match at Bournemouth – the hottest ever temperature recorded in Britain.

At least we were by the seaside and the pavilion staff kept the iced limes coming for the sweltering hacks as sweat dripped onto notebooks and over laptops.

The game itself was over all too quickly, the county collapsing to another two-day defeat and Lamb was offering up no excuses.

Some pride was restored at Chesterfield's leafy Queen's Park ground, a beautiful cricketing outpost.

The match ended in a draw, Northamptonshire finishing ten runs short of victory and two wickets short of defeat. **145**

It was entertaining fare with that man Capel again in the sweetest touch and going potty with the bat in the first innings.

He got after former England spinner Geoff Miller in particular, hitting eight sixes and eight fours in a wonderfully entertaining innings which saw the ball fished out of the flower beds on more than one occasion.

Capel said: "I was struggling with my back and my ankle but got wheeled out at Chesterfield.

"I was heavily bandaged up and scored a hundred and a fifty in the game with minimal running involved!"

## V FOR VICTORY AT NORTHLANDS ROAD

It was back to Hampshire soon after, for a stunning NatWest semi-final encounter at Southampton's Northlands Road ground.

Allan Lamb lost the toss on this occasion but his 'bat them out of sight' plan was still intact when Mark Nicholas invited the county to take first strike.

Northamptonshire blitzed their way to 284 all out from their 60 overs with Lamb, Larkins, Williams and Capel all making useful runs but Malcolm Marshall and David Gower threatened to take the tie away from the county.

Hampshire however were bowled out for 283 off the final ball in the gathering south coast dusk, Mark Robinson keeping his cool in a fine final over which sealed the deal, and a trip to Lord's, by one run.

It evoked memories of the thrilling matches from 1981, and for me this was one of the greatest games of one-day cricket.

Capel was hauled over the coals for, shall we say, over-enthusiastically inviting Gower to depart the field after taking the catch to dismiss the stylish left-hander off the bowling of Williams.                                                                    **146**

Capel recalled the day: "For some reason we were sitting watching our innings from the Hampshire balcony and it was all a bit uncomfortable.

"Malcolm Marshall was bowling early on and the ball did a lot in the first hour or so, probably more than it did in the final at Lord's.

"Marshall could easily have had us 30-5 but somehow we stuck in there and the ball stayed clear of the edge.

"During their innings, Gower and Marshall came together and were definitely having a bit of luck.

"Amby missed one at long-off, the crowd were a bit naughty, Lamby missed another off me and I thought it was going to be a case of the Nottinghamshire 1987 final all over again.

"I got really pumped up and was moved to field at long-off. Gower sent one straight down my throat, a real pressure catch situation. The crowd were doing their best to put me off but I hung on, threw the ball in the air and gestured towards Gower to move on.

"Mark Robinson held his nerve again at the death as he had done against Worcestershire in the previous round and, in the dusk, we won a fantastic game of cricket.

"The headlines should have been all about our performance and the match, instead it was all about my incident with Gower.

"I wanted to celebrate our win but a TCCB chap wanted to have a little chat. I ended up being severely censured but not fined."

Felton said: "Mark Robinson's last over was absolutely fantastic, I think he bowled 56, 58 and 60 and kept it very tight under pressure. Curtly I think was more expensive.

"I remember catching Bobby Parks in the deep and not seeing the ball until very late. It was one of the best games I've ever played in.

"When we'd batted first I'd got hit by Malcolm Marshall, which wasn't pleasant!" **147**

Coverdale added: "We'd sneaked home in a thrilling finale against Worcestershire and then had to travel to play Hampshire at Southampton in the semi.

"Hampshire had Malcolm Marshall, David Gower and Robin Smith in their ranks and a wonderful game of cricket came down to the last over which was bowled by Mark Robinson.

"The odds were very much in Hampshire's favour and I said something to chairman Lynn Wilson along the lines of 'Sorry chairman. We've come so close, but not close enough'.

"Hampshire needed two to win off the last ball and PJ Bakker was at the crease. Bakker hit it to cover, Allan Lamb fielded it and, as he ran in, he lobbed the ball in to David Ripley behind the stumps.

"Ever since I've had occasional nightmares that Rips dropped the throw in but thankfully he'd bagged it, effected the run-out, and we'd claimed a fantastic victory. We celebrated long into the night.

"However the Gower incident when, after catching him out, Capes gave Gower a V-sign that was caught on television, had us in hot water with the TCCB again.

"I had Tony Brown on the phone the next day for a disciplinary chat and was then also made aware that Oslear had cited us for about 25 separate offences of breaching advertising regulations in another match on TV! Talk about the umpire fights back!"

There is little room for sentiment in sport these days but one pleasant exception took place at Wantage Road towards the end of August.

Geoff Cook and Wayne Larkins – for so long a marriage made in heaven at the top of the Northamptonshire batting order – took their final bow as an opening pair in a Sunday match against Gloucestershire, in light of Cook's retirement.

Together with a tribute to the late Colin Milburn, it made for an emotional day. And Northamptonshire won by two runs! **148**

The home Championship match with Essex brought with it some drama, with Winston Davis – on a rare outing – steaming in to bowl to England skipper Graham Gooch.

Davis said: "I didn't have a happy season in 1990. The pendulum had gone the other way, from having too much cricket I suddenly felt I wasn't getting enough.

"This left me feeling undervalued, I certainly felt the club's selectors were favouring Ambrose and I didn't think that was fair because I didn't think he was better than me.

"Matters came to a head in this match, Gooch was in his pomp and I was running in to bowl to him. My first ball he smacked through the covers almost disdainfully and I wasn't having that. The next two I dug in short to get him on the back foot and the fourth ball I pitched up to him, striking him full on the pad in front of all three stumps.

"Up went the appeal and I turned to umpire Kevin Lyons who didn't lift his finger. I turned to Gooch who was looking at his feet still in front of the stumps and, I think, feeling rather uncomfortable.

"I couldn't believe he hadn't been given out and I wasn't happy. I stood my ground and Lamby came down from the slips in an attempt to placate me.

"Lamby could be an irritant at times and he certainly was on this occasion.

"I think I expected some support from my team captain but, although I can't remember what he said exactly, I didn't feel the support was forthcoming.

"Lamby was good mates with Gooch, he was his vice-captain on the tour to the West Indies earlier that year.

"He got me annoyed and I shouted something like 'I can't believe this' so loud that I think someone may have heard me down in Northampton town centre!

"It seemed like an hour had gone by before I finally bowled the fifth ball of the over.

"Needless to say, I was hauled up before the committee to answer a charge of dissent.

"It was inevitable, as that year there had been already been conduct issues with Ambrose against Reeve and then Capel against Gower.

"But it was the final straw for me. I told the committee that I would not be returning to the club, and that was that."

## THE BATTING PLAN GOES AWRY...

And so arrived Nat West Final day, once again Northamptonshire batting first after losing the toss.

But there was to be no run bonanza on this occasion, a sticky 10.30am September start and a fired-up Phil DeFreitas landing the county in all sorts of early trouble.

From 30-5 in the first hour or so, Northamptonshire made a stuttering recovery to 171 all out but it was never realistically going to be enough against a strong Lancashire outfit.

Ambrose top-scored for 48 and was ably assisted by Capel in ensuring respectability.

Capel said: "We lost the toss and were put in with conditions favouring the bowlers. There was a little bit in the pitch in the first hour and DeFreitas bowled a very good line and length and did just enough.

"It was his day, fair play to him. Three days before the final I had broken my finger but I was determined to play.

"I wasn't at full capacity, it wasn't easy, but I managed to get some runs on the board with Curtly who batted superbly.

"Things weren't really going for us. Neil Fairbrother played a very important innings for Lancashire and he was missed at mid-on by Curtly. He then chanced his arm and played a match-winning innings to win them the final."

Felton recalled: "The final was a massive let-down, we were in big trouble in the first hour and never really recovered enough to where we needed to be. **150**

"There's a saying that goes 'play the game and not the occasion' and unfortunately Lancashire played the game and we let the occasion get to us.

"Capes and Ambrose actually got us to a respectable score.

"They got on well together and had a very good relationship. Capes looked after him a bit.

"They gave us half a chance and we might even had won it but for one error in the field. Neil Fairbrother went down the track to Nick Cook and hit the ball straight at Curtly. Unfortunately, the ball hit Curtly on the knee and the catch went begging."

Coverdale added: "After the start we made I wanted to crawl into a hole and disappear but we managed to pull the score round so that we at least had a defendable total on the board.

"The match turned when Curtly Ambrose dropped Neil Fairbrother, the best one-day player around at the time.

"Fairbrother was in early against the new ball which was a key part of our game plan and we needed to take that chance.

"He was let off and steered them through. I think we would have won if Curtly had taken the catch."

Northamptonshire didn't wallow in the Lord's blues for too long, travelling to play Essex in Chelmsford where the side notched up a massive 276-run victory.

The first innings was a struggle but the batsmen blossomed second time around with Fordham, Bailey and Lamb all celebrating centuries in a score of 636-6.

Then Ambrose put Essex's up-and-coming Aussie batsman Mark Waugh to the sword, producing an unplayable snorter which had him caught in the slips by Lamb.

It was a memorable delivery and showcased the West Indian quickie at his very best.                **151**

The final game of the season was just up the road at Grace Road and Northamptonshire finished up with another resounding win to conclude a season that was more down than up. In a great year for batsmen, it was interesting to note that Lamb didn't actually play that much cricket for the county during 1990 and that was clearly reflected in the mid-term results.

Before the year was out, Robinson also announced he was going home – to his native Yorkshire. Cook left the club and returned to his native Durham to embark on their odyssey into the big time and Larkins was dropped from the vice-captaincy in favour of skipper-elect Bailey.

In a year most batsmen made hay, Capel averaged 65.36 with the bat and his bowling average came in at 27.35.


## PRETORIA ON NENE

The disappointment of 1990 resulted in far-reaching changes within the club and Lamb enlisted the help of South African legend Mike Procter to assist him in a director of cricket role. West Indian paceman Eldine Baptiste was signed up, with Davis having departed and Ambrose on tour with the West Indies in England.

Rookie left-armer Paul Taylor was snapped up from Staffordshire but most of the headlines centred on the recruitment of a talented Zimbabwean all-rounder from Gloucestershire, Kevin Curran.

Coverdale said: "Mike Procter was our first director of cricket, recruited by me and Peter Arnold at the request of Allan Lamb. When Mike met us for the first time we knew within moments that he was the right man for us.

"A warm-up game took us to Cambridge University. I was with Mike at Fenners and recall him observing Paul Taylor in that match and declaring there and then that Taylor would one day play for England." **152**

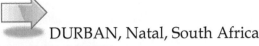 DURBAN, Natal, South Africa

MIKE PROCTER

Born: 15 September 1946

Northamptonshire: 1991 to 1992

RHB/RF

Taylor had gone for 92 runs off 12 overs in the NatWest Trophy match against Northamptonshire the previous year, so Taylor's move to Wantage Road naturally raised quite a few eyebrows!

Coverdale added: "Taylor had been released by Derbyshire a year or two earlier, a decision which surprised our coach Bob Carter who rated him.

"Yes he went for a lot of runs in the Trophy game but we didn't see the figures.

"What we took note of was the way he ran in tirelessly, the way he fielded and the fact that a lot of the runs conceded came off edges and nicks.

"We needed a left-armer in our attack – young Simon Brown had left and Gareth Smith had not progressed in the way we hoped.

"So I rang Taylor in the middle of the night, as he was playing club cricket for Kalgoorlie in Western Australia.

I told him we were prepared to take a punt on him – my phone call came completely out of the blue so he was pretty gob smacked by this development!"

And then there was Curran, who was courted by lots of other counties but opted for a new lease of life at Northampton.

Coverdale said: "Twelve counties at least were interested in getting the so-called bad boy of English cricket, Kevin Curran.

"Other counties were mentioned ahead of us but I thought we had a pretty good chance of getting him. **153**

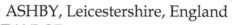ASHBY, Leicestershire, England
PAUL TAYLOR
Born: 8 August 1964
Northamptonshire: 1991 to 2001
LHB/LFM

"Eventually I drove down to Clifton in Bristol and he agreed to sign the paperwork there and then. I know that Mark Nicholas from Hampshire had also been down to see him earlier that day and apparently he let it be known that Kevin would be signing for them!

"Although the papers were signed we had to wait a while before we could officially lodge his registration.

"It was quite amusing because during this waiting period, Lynn Wilson and I had gone across to watch the Coventry v Liverpool football match at Highfield Road.

"The then Warwickshire chairman Bob Evans was our host on that day and he was constantly chatting to us, telling us how he was also confident of landing Curran.

"Lynn and I kept silent on the subject but really we were bursting to tell Bob that the deal had already had been done and he was coming to Northamptonshire. When we finally left we had a good laugh about the matter!

"Curran had a great deal of respect for Lamby and was keen to play for him. To be honest I never had a problem with him, maybe the odd issue around dress code aside. He was truly committed to doing well.

"I remember driving with Kevin at the very end of the 1991 season, his first with us, and him telling me that he enjoyed being part of the group and that this had been the best year of his cricketing life.

"He personally thanked me which was really good of him – he certainly didn't need to do so. **154**

RUSAPE, Manicaland, Zimbabwe
KEVIN CURRAN
Born: 7 September 1959
Death: 10 October 2012
Northamptonshire: 1991 to 1998
Nickname: KC
RHB/RFM

"Kevin wanted to do very well in cricket and very well in life. He was driven and ambitious and his premature death stopped us all in our tracks."

Felton said: "Mike Procter arrived during the winter and so too Kevin Curran.

"Procter persevered with Fordham and Larkins and it was a poor season for me, although in the back of my mind was the fact that Larkins would be following Cook to Durham at the end of the summer.

"Another new arrival was Paul Taylor from Staffordshire. What a signing he proved to be, a wicket-taking left-armer who helped Capes out quite a bit in terms of easing the workload.

"The Curran and Capel partnership got off to a bad start. Curran's arrival knocked Capes who clearly saw him as a threat.

"I saw it that we had two excellent all-round cricketers in our middle order and Capes should not have felt the way he did."

Capel acknowledged Curran's abilities. He said: "He certainly maximised what talent he had and he had an incredible amount of self-belief.

"He was always a man with a plan, sometimes it worked and sometimes it didn't. But it never stopped him believing in himself!                                                                         **155**

"We both had our professional pride, and while there was a rivalry between us it was a healthy one."

Ripley said: "When Kevin Curran came on the scene at the start of the 1990s, we had two cricketing all-rounders of top quality in him and Capes.

"The contrast between them at the crease was quite distinct. Capes always looked graceful when he prepared to bat, Kevin's stance wasn't so – let's call it gutsy.

"At six and seven in the side, their contribution together over the years was quite even."

Capel and wife Debbie were beset by personal tragedy early in May when their baby daughter Laura died shortly after birth.

Coverdale said: "This was a difficult and traumatic year for David and Debbie.

"I went to see them that same evening and David was in bits. Lamby and his wife Lindsay were a tremendous support to him at this time.

"It was hard for everyone at the club. Spectators only see the professional cricketer, easily forgetting that behind the sporting face is a human side having to deal with the ups and downs of family and private life.

"Alongside this personal tragedy, David didn't really take the signing of Kevin Curran well.

"He felt that Kevin had come in on a huge amount of extra money, which I can assure you wasn't the case, but there was a certain amount of coolness on David's part."

On the field, Northamptonshire had got off to a steady start under Procter, who attributed an early spate of pulled muscles and strains to a heavily-sanded Wantage Road pitch – the groundstaff disagreed!

An early home Sunday game with Hampshire saw Northamptonshire smash 280-4 from their 40 overs, Bailey scoring 47 of them off just 19 deliveries.

The West Indian tourist fixture saw the focus switch on Lamb, Curran and Thomas for different reasons.  **156**

There was much speculation about Lamb's England future, now that he was no longer Gooch's deputy.

Also scoring well in the speculation stakes were stories about Curran's alleged earnings.

While his salary was pretty much in line with others in the club, it was suggested that Curran was benefiting from a considerable number of spin-offs and add-ons.

And Thomas, the world's fastest white bowler, was to pit his wits against the Windies quicks - he was reticent about the whole thing and in the match itself the visitors took his bowling apart.


## CARVED IN STONE

There was some light relief in the NatWest Trophy first round match with Staffordshire in Stone, a return to his native potteries for Bailey and a return to his former county for Taylor.

Bailey had been tagged the Biddulph Blaster by my predecessor and blast away he jolly well did in the Potteries, hammering 145 runs in a comfortable Northamptonshire victory.

As the Chronicle & Echo headline ran the following day, 'Bailey's epitaph carved in Stone'.

Bailey said: "I enjoyed my only playing return to Staffordshire. I won the man-of-the-match award but I didn't think it would pan out like that at the start of the game.

"Alan Fordham and Nigel Felton were opening and I replaced Felton, who had a ball fly off a length which I think he gloved to slip. I went out there thinking that the pitch could be an interesting one but that was the only ball that misbehaved all day.

"We'd played Staffordshire at Northampton the previous year and Paul Taylor went for big runs - and we ended up signing him!                                    **157**

"Most of us naturally had some doubts as to the wisdom of this move but those doubts were completely misplaced.

"Paul was one of those bowlers who could run in all day and he was also a great fielder - an excellent asset to the side and of course he went on to play for England.

"So it just goes to show that stats are not everything and whoever recommended him to the club deserves a very big pat on the back!"

What would otherwise have been a routine trip to play Kent at Mote Park in Maidstone was enlivened by news from the County Ground nets, where reports suggested there had been a bust up during practice between Greg Thomas and Kevin Curran.

And an anonymous letter was subsequently received by the club, criticising the way the club was being run.

The identity of the letter writer was never established but Thomas was perceived as the culprit and, from that moment on, there was a clear distance between the fast bowler and the Wantage Road hierarchy.

Strangely enough, his future appearances for the club were limited and he only played when Bailey was skipper, not Lamb!

The county went down to a heavy defeat with the quality of the pitch proving deceptive and Procter engaged me in a long chat about the responsible role of the press as the 'nets bust up' story hit home.

Worse was to follow as the Mail On Sunday then picked up on the anonymous letter story, which naturally suggested there was trouble at mill.

That afternoon, during the Sunday match at Tring, Procter convened a press conference for the local media to discuss the situation.

Tring was losing its charm among the local scribes, the venue now described as the 'Hertfordshire hell hole' and one which was soon to disappear from the calendar although, in many ways, it was a sad loss.                                    **158**

Back in the NatWest, Northamptonshire entertained rivals Leicestershire and the visitors amassed a testing 255-6 from their 60 overs.

But in the end they were no match for the home side who totalled 259-1, with Fordham celebrating a brilliant unbeaten 132 - Procter was full of praise for the young opener's prolific contribution to the side.

Procter was now being talked about loudly as the chosen new boss of South Africa, who were due to return to the cricketing family the following year.

This meant uncertainty all round in respect of the county futures of not only Procter but also Lamb, Larkins, Thomas and Ambrose.

On the morning of the final day of a drawn match against Middlesex at Uxbridge, habitually boring, I was summoned to captain Allan Lamb's table at breakfast.

Lamb, quite pleasantly, stated his case in respect of the Chronicle & Echo's coverage of Northamptonshire cricket, referencing the nets bust up and anonymous letter saga.

Lamb was concerned that the newspaper was feeding off disruptive sources around the club.

A bunker mentality had clearly set in and Lamb, on a number of fronts, clearly felt a little unsettled.

Certain elements of his team were at loggerheads, his England future was uncertain and his friend and mentor looked like he would be on the move.

The visit of Nottinghamshire to Wellingborough School was over in two days as Franklyn Stephenson, once on Northamptonshire's books wreaked havoc with Andy Pick.

So much so that the extra hour was claimed on day two and Northamptonshire were duly finished off on the Saturday evening. It was a remarkable day with the county out of the running at lunchtime but back to even-stevens at tea.

Then Nottinghamshire's last pair held up proceedings, before the county batsmen slumped to 68 all out, losing by an innings and one run.

A case of '68 Crash' – not quite the Suzi Quatro hit, but apologies anyway – and you had to feel for Evening Telegraph reporter Steve Harrison.

He had sneaked off home at teatime with the match evenly poised only to turn on teletext later that evening to discover that the match was over!

It resulted in him frantically cribbing some notes and statistics so that he could meet his Monday morning deadline!

The fixture planners were having a chuckle when they asked Northamptonshire to fulfil a fixture against Sussex at Eastbourne and then hike overnight to the next match, Lancashire at Lytham!

The Lytham trip however was an opportunity for two young players to take their place in the sun, and Neil Stanley and namesake Andy Roberts did so in style.

Stanley whacked a career-best 132 and leg-spinner Roberts followed that up with 6-72, also a career best, in a fine win.

Even Lamb made his mark on the match in quite a different way, bowling and taking a couple of wickets... not forgetting 125 with the bat!

And so the NatWest odyssey lined up another semi-final, with Northamptonshire squaring up to Surrey at The Oval which had a reasonable crowd in and for once actually had a bit of life about the place.

A tense affair carried over into two days, with Surrey scoring 208-8 off 60 overs. Northamptonshire were 22 runs adrift of victory when bad light stopped play at the end of day one, closing on 187-8 with Waqar Younis, tail up, fizzing the ball around in deadly fashion.

After much indecision from Lamb in the pavilion, Curran and Taylor were eventually summoned in to fight another day.

Curran's tenure with Northamptonshire remained a source of great controversy and many of the national media commentators had taken against him.

Northamptonshire were quickly dismissed on the next morning's resumption when the weather was distinctly brighter, but the dark mood in the press box prevailed.

When Curran lost his wicket, nationals scribe Michael Henderson raced to the front of the Oval press box and banged on the window pane to signal his pleasure at the dismissal!

Coverdale said: "We didn't pull up any trees in the Championship in 1991 although we had a good run in the Sunday League.

"However we did well again in the NatWest and were involved in a controversial semi-final against Surrey at The Oval when we came off for bad light at the end of the first day when we needed about 20 to win with two wickets left.

"There was a full house there and we took a lot of stick for coming off when we did but it was totally unplayable for it was very dark.

"Sadly we lost a wicket at the very start of the next day and finished just short. However it was still the right decision."

Surrey were the Championship visitors soon afterwards and Lamb put them to the sword.

However Lamb needed the assistance of a runner in the later stages of the innings – Richard Montgomerie obliged – and, when six runs short of a double century, Montgomerie contrived to get run out.

And there was a salutary lesson for yours truly in the late-season match with Gloucestershire at Bristol, that most sociable of cricketing outposts. I had just started wearing contact lenses – memo to self, if you are wearing lenses make sure you look after them properly if you go out for a drink.

One evening the hotel room was spinning but I had remembered to remove said lenses before retiring to bed.

And I recalled getting up a few times in the night for a couple of glasses of water to ease a parched throat and aching head, then back to bed.

In the morning, I vainly searched for the lenses which were not in their case. Only to remember that I'd left the lenses in a glass of water in the bathroom.

And with that the creeping and shocking realisation that I'd downed a few glasses of water during the night and had managed to drink my contact lenses!

On organising replacement lenses, this in the day when disposables weren't all the rage as they are now, I'm not sure whether the optician quite believed me when I told her how I had come to be without lenses…

Never a dull moment in Bristol. And, to this day, every time I put my contact lenses in, the good old Unicorn Hotel is never far from my mind. And I'm always wary about drinking a glass of water!

For the record, Northamptonshire recorded another fine victory in this match which made it four Championship wins from the last six.

Defeat followed in the final game of the season against Warwickshire at Edgbaston, as much dominated by matters off the field as on it.

The retained list was out and it was farewell to Eldine Baptiste who was released, Wayne Larkins, who joined his old buddy Geoff Cook (and also Ian Botham and Dean Jones) at Durham and Greg Thomas, who retired.

Also retiring was Thomas's old friend and sparring partner Winston Davis, who had spent one year in the Yorkshire League with Skipton after leaving Northamptonshire.

He said: "I returned to St Vincent but, after my accident in 1998, I came back to England and now live in Worcestershire.

"As a young cricketer in St Vincent, gaining recognition was difficult because the selectors would often favour the big boys like Barbados, Jamaica and Trinidad and Tobago.

"I was surprised to be selected for the Young West Indies teams against Young England in 1976 and 1978. **162**

"But I should have played more for the West Indies. I held my own against the star cricketers at the time but there were certain attitudes prevailing at the top of West Indies cricket at the time and it was hard for me to make my mark.

"But you can't keep a good man down, and I certainly lit a few fires under a few backsides in my time!

"One of my fondest memories was beating Barbados in the Shell Shield on their own Kensington Oval with the likes of Desmond Haynes, Malcolm Marshall, Joel Garner and Wayne Daniel in their team.

"And I also chuckle when I recall a game for the Windward Islands against Guyana in Dominica.

"Guyana had the great Clive Lloyd at the crease. I was fielding at mid-off and I couldn't help but notice Lloyd backing up too far out of his crease as our off-spinner, Stanley Hinds, came in to bowl.

"Lloyd did this a few times and I had a quiet word with Hinds who then ran him out. Lloyd never let me forget this!

"Lloyd of course is one of the greats of the game and with him you have to put Sir Vivian Richards.

"As a batsman he was just special. There was no predictability about him, he played with a certain arrogance and dismissiveness which he could get away with.

"I remember the West Indies in Australia, when they had Dennis Lillee, Jeff Thomson and Len Pascoe all firing in and fancying their chances.

"They started out with four slips, two gullies and a cover point and had us at 5-2.

"In came Richards and the close field just evaporated as they switched to two slips, a gully and an extra cover!

"Desmond Haynes was the complete opening batsman with tremendous technique and Malcolm Marshall the complete fast bowler.

"Marshall could swing the ball, cut the ball, bounce the ball, skid the ball, he had the lot. And he didn't like you getting forward to him, woe betide if you did that! **163**

"Andy Roberts was another fast bowler I admired, especially his pace and his unerring accuracy."

"I still see Gordon Greenidge from time to time, also Courtney Walsh and Phil Simmons in Bristol.

"Curtly Ambrose I'm not really in touch with but he will always look to support me by playing for Lashings and in benefit cricket.

"Roger Harper I also haven't seen for a while. He was another player who didn't really fulfil his potential.

"He wasn't a big spinner of the ball but at Test level he was a phenomenal fielder and he was a better batter than his record indicates.

"He was the cousin of Clive Lloyd and that created some tension in the West Indies team, especially when Harper was being tipped as the next captain of the West Indies.

"With big hitters like Sir Viv Richards and Gordon Greenidge still around, this was a weight on his shoulders.

"With Harper, as with Ramnaresh Sarwan more recently, the argument was the same – are they good enough to be in the team let alone lead the team?

"I have a lot of time for Sarwan. I think he is a good cricketer and he certainly deserved his place in the national side."

And what future lies ahead for the West Indies side now, no longer at the top table of international cricket?

Davis added: "West Indies cricket has declined in recent years but I don't think it's down to the fact that the islands no longer produce any quality players.

"I think the quality is there and I don't put it down to young sportsmen being distracted by other more lucrative sports to pursue.

"In my opinion, the cricketers coming through these days no longer have a respect for or an understanding of the game.

"West Indies cricket is unique in that the national team draws from several island communities.

**164**

"These islands do not command the same financial backing as say England, Australia and India.

"I remember speaking to West Indies chief Steve Camacho and asking him why Australia kept all the profit from a series in which the Australian public had turned out to see a West Indies team at the height of its powers.

"I asked the question – they are coming to see us play, why don't we get the money?

"For 15 years the West Indies were the best team in the world and we drew big crowds when we toured. But we have never had the clout to make sure we got a good financial deal.

"When it comes to attracting sponsorship, and it is a straight choice between England and the West Indies, the commercial backing will always go England's way.

"It has always been the same over the years. It is a prejudice and a bias, it is covert, but it is there.

"There is petty rivalry between the islands, between cricket officials and cricket spectators. It is borne out of insularity.

"West Indian crowds are very knowledgeable about their cricket and this rivalry and insularity will emerge if they feel a cricketer in the national team is not doing what they feel needs to be done. If you're not performing the way they want you to, they will get on your tail.

"West Indians like to see action, no matter what the state of the game. Even if you are batting and are 50-6, they expect you to have a go to the end."


## THE 'FOUR FOR' AT FORFAR

Before the domestic season got underway in 1992, the Cricket World Cup took place in Australia with Lamb representing Northamptonshire interests.

England beat Australia in Sydney and also South Africa in Melbourne before losing to Pakistan in the final.  **165**

One of Northamptonshire's opening forays was an away trip to Scotland in the Benson & Hedges Cup, which took them to the unlikely cricketing outpost of Forfar.

It was a surreal experience, watching county cricket with the Highlands, still snow-capped in places, visible in the background. And it was cold.

Former county spinner Jimmy Govan, representing his country, took 'four for' in Forfar but it wasn't enough to stave off defeat for his home nation.

Alan Fordham blasted 192 against Surrey at Wantage Road and most observes felt that at England opportunity could now not be far away.

The history books will now tell you otherwise but Capel said: "Alan Fordham was a very good county opener and averaged 40 throughout his career, which speaks for itself.

"At the rate which he scored, particularly in three-day cricket, he placed us in many positive positions which helped us to win a lot of games.

"He took the attack to the opposition. He was good on the front foot, strong on the back through the offside and had a good pull shot.

"A really top man, he performed really well in his role as an opening batsman and has gone on to serve magnificently well with the English Cricket Board."

Durham played their first season in the County Championship in 1992 and one of the first sides they entertained were Northamptonshire, who made a three-day Championship visit to Stockton-on-Tees.

Another quirk of the fixture was the fact that Wayne Larkins was now lining up against the county where he had made his name.

Capel said: "Playing against Ned was in some ways an unusual experience, bowling to one of my favourite long-standing team-mates. I managed to get him out on a 50-50 lbw shout. Ned needed to score a century to complete his full set against all the counties. **166**

"He didn't do it on this occasion but did so in a later game at Northampton."

Experience told as Northamptonshire enforced the follow-on against their hosts and went on to win by eight wickets in a dramatic finale.

With only a few overs left in the game, and quick runs needed, Northamptonshire opened with Allan Lamb and Alan Fordham to take the match.

Lamb was again in complete control in a Sunday match at home to Sussex, flaying the south coast side's bowlers to all parts in completing a 48-ball century.

And Lamb, Fordham and Ambrose were all on their game as Northamptonshire brushed aside Yorkshire in the second round of the NatWest Trophy, by an emphatic 133 runs at Wantage Road.

Lamb was at it again in the home Championship match with Warwickshire, contributing 209 out of a county score of 307.

But the Bears somehow failed to win the game, which seemed to be comfortably attainable as the final 20 overs clicked round on the last day.

It was Rob Bailey who proved the match-winner as Northamptonshire got past Glamorgan at Swansea in the NatWest quarter-final.

Felton recalled: "Rob batted slowly, too slowly some thought at the time, but he finished with 98 not out to enable us to get a defendable total on the board.

"Glamorgan of course had Viv Richards, who presented a massive threat to our progress in the competition, but it was David Capel who got him out, caught behind for two, and we won comfortably!"

Capel said of Bailey: "He started out as a natural number five, a dominant front-foot player who liked hitting the ball down the ground and scoring quick hundreds.

"The next step was to move up to number three, which meant him adapting to building longer innings.      **167**

"He had to change his approach and play in a more responsible manner which he did very well, particularly in 1987 when pitches had a bit more grass on and the top order had to work harder."

Slow left-armer Nick Cook found his bowling performance had come under close scrutiny and his captain was particularly critical.

So he was delighted to get his bowling back on track with a match-winning performance over Essex at Chelmsford and made his feelings quite clear in an emotional post-match interview!

There were several noteworthy inputs as Northamptonshire defeated Hampshire at Bournemouth early on the final day.

Lamb scored 160, in the process denting his own car on the boundary edge with a big six, and Kevin Curran claimed 6-45 in the home side's first innings.

Paul Taylor went one better on the final afternoon - the ball swung around merrily for the left-armer in favourable conditions and he returned figures of 7-23, including four wickets in one over!

A tough NatWest semi draw paired Northamptonshire with their old adversaries Warwickshire at Edgbaston.

The Brumbrella took centre stage as the start was delayed because of rain but when play did get underway, the hosts were dismissed for 149. But the game was far from over, with the whirlwind Allan Donald posing a considerable threat to the county's fortunes.

The game crept into a second day and required a steady hand to see the job through. And the steady hand was provided by Nigel Felton, who registered his best performance for Northamptonshire and provided the anchor to secure another Lord's final.

Felton said: "At this stage of the season, the captain was out of the Test picture and he was concentrated on the side which had a settled and balanced look and feel about it.  **168**

"We enjoyed a very good season and the NatWest Trophy was the clear highlight.

"This was a tough draw and the rain ensured it was a stop-start game from the off.

"We bowled well to keep them in check, everyone bowling very tightly, but getting the runs was never going to be easy, especially with Allan Donald charging in and often in very poor light.

"We were 47-2 overnight chasing 150 – Lamby and I were at the crease - and I remember not getting very much sleep that night.

"I stuck around for a half-century which was enough to get us home by three wickets.

"I was out just before the end but was delighted to win the man-of-the-match award which got us to Lord's once more.

"I was especially pleased with the innings and result because it was in this particular match that I was aware of a fault with my batting technique.

"Alan Fordham had pointed it out and said I was making life difficult for myself at the crease.

"I was very conscious of that. During the winter that followed I worked on getting things right when I was out in Cape Town, coaching with Forders and Wayne Noon.

"In those days a Lord's final was still very much an occasion. This time we were determined to make sure we approached the game differently to the one against Lancashire two years previously."

Coverdale said: "This was Mike Procter's second year and I felt we were on the verge of being a good side.

"The NatWest Trophy success was the undoubted highlight and we had a tough semi-final against Warwickshire at Edgbaston, where Jeremy Snape had to play and was thrust into the side unexpectedly due to illness.

"Nigel Felton played magnificently, especially against Allan Donald who was bowling at the speed of light. **169**

"We could have been blown away on the first evening but Felts held firm.

"I had to be at Lord's for a meeting the next day and the news came through very late that we had actually won the game! Sitting in the meeting for hours, not knowing the result at Edgbaston, was purgatory!"

A tense draw at home to Kent in the Championship – which effectively saw Northamptonshire's title hopes slip away – gave little indication of the on-field and off-field drama to follow in the weeks ahead.

There were lawyers as well as journalists in the Wantage Road press box for the Middlesex game, the opening day of which became known as 'Allan Lamb day'.

Now out of the England picture, Lamb, together with Ian Botham, had gone public with allegations about Pakistan's ball tampering practices, referencing former county favourite Sarfraz Nawaz as they pointed the finger.

Lamb was promptly suspended by the club, but the suspension had lifted in time for the NatWest Final against Leicestershire.

Coverdale takes up the story. He said: "A few weeks before the final, England had played Pakistan in a one-day international series and allegations that Pakistan players routinely tampered with the ball were rife.

"We were due to hold a cricket committee meeting at the ground one evening. Lamby rang me on his way back from being with the England squad, ostensibly to find out what time the meeting was to take place.

"His last words in that call were 'We could be in for a bit of fun, I've given my views on ball tampering.' Frankly I didn't realise the significance of those words at the time.

"When he finally came in to the committee meeting, some while after it had started, Lamby asked for the club's fax number and a little while later a proof of the Daily Mirror's article about the matter, quoting Lamby, appeared over the fax. **170**

"Lynn Wilson and I were very concerned and Lynn rang Lamby up and asked him if it was too late to get the article pulled. It transpired it was too late, it had gone to print and Lynn and I knew immediately we had to take action against our captain before the Test and County Cricket Board did.

"There were lots of phone calls that night and we got together with Mike Procter very early the next morning and the decision was taken to suspend Lamby for two matches.

"Tony Brown from the TCCB was on our case but they were satisfied that we had taken the appropriate action and at least we had Lamby available for the NatWest final.

"To this day though it still staggers me as to the volume of hate mail we received at the club, some really abusive stuff.

"Lamby, me, the chairman, the club, we were all judged to be racists! There was no end to it!

"One letter still sticks with me, a rather scruffy envelope and scrawled on the back it said 'you and Jacques Delors should be put in a bag and dumped in the middle of the English Channel'.

"Delors at that time was a big player in the European Union and not much liked by the Government of the day. Probably the one and only time I'll be mentioned in the same breath as Jacques Delors!"

## OUR STAR BOWLER HAS BEEN KIDNAPPED!

The final itself was sniffed at by commentators who pointed out that a match between two unfashionable Midlands counties was registering little box office interest.

Dull, dull, dull…. and while the on-field stuff turned out to be pretty routine, the peripherals proved to be far from routine!

The night before the match, Northamptonshire feared their star fast bowler had been kidnapped by the military arm of the 'green ink' brigade.

**171**

And just before the match got underway, there was to be more action of the legal variety!

The drama began as the players gathered for their pre-final dinner in the team hotel on the Friday night.

Capel said: "After training at Lord's that afternoon we were aware that we were missing one of our key team members!

"Curtly didn't turn up for the session and as we sat down for dinner later on he still hadn't arrived.

"Secretary Steve Coverdale was understandably getting concerned at this point, thinking he may be in some sort of trouble, and started hitting the phones.

"We'd just finished the main course when Curtly, in his inimitable style, suddenly walked into the room, flashed a smile, and said 'Good evening gentlemen, I believe I'm a little late!'

"He then sat down and it's fair to say that everyone was pleased to see him and whatever tension was there lifted for Steve!"

Coverdale recalled: "For the final we were staying in a different hotel than we usually stayed in for Lord's trips.

"It was a new hotel on the cricket circuit at that time, although it is used regularly by teams visiting headquarters nowadays. The players had been to Lord's to drop off their kit – one or two of them had a practice session too - and the evening before the match we'd organised a team meal for 8pm.

"Everything was fine apart from the fact that Curtly Ambrose hadn't turned up and after some considerable time there was still no sign of him.

"We were all getting worried that something had happened to him. We phoned his house - no answer – so we sent someone round there to find it deserted and we talked about phoning the police because, in light of the Pakistani ball tampering row, we thought someone may have targeted him and kidnapped him.  **172**

"We checked the AA and RAC to find out if there had been any accidents on the M1. But there was nothing for them to report.

"He eventually walked into the dining room with a smile and an apology. He had apparently arrived in London only to discover that his partner had left the tickets they required back in Northampton. So they had driven back to get them!"

Before the start of play on the day of the final, Sarfraz Nawaz hijacked the occasion by having a writ ceremoniously served upon Allan Lamb in connection with the ball tampering allegations.

When the match got underway and resulted in an eight-wicket victory for Northamptonshire, the relief in anti-climactically clinching a first trophy in 12 years was almost palpable.

And there was a lot of joy because this day had been a long time in coming. As it turned out, the 1992 NatWest Trophy would remain Northamptonshire's last major trophy for another 21 years.

But at least it provided some sort of return for a very talented cricket team.

Man of the match was man of the season Alan Fordham, who got after Leicestershire again with a match-winning 91.

Capel said: "At lunchtime, the feeling in the dressing room was that it had been Leicestershire's morning and that we had to turn things around.

"As often happens in these types of matches, they get turned by one moment of inspiration and that was provided by Kevin Curran with a magnificent run out.

"KC picked up the ball, taking the batter out to break the stumps and run out Tim Boon.

"He literally threw himself on the line that day, his will to win was immense.

"That enabled us to get one end open and apply pressure as a bowling unit to restrict them to a low total on a slow pitch. **173**

"Excellent batting partnerships between Fordham and Bailey, and later Bailey and Lamb, resulted in a secure feeling in the dressing room as we reached the total comfortably.

"It was another top-line performance from Fordham, which won him the man-of-the-match award."

Fordham's opening batting partner Felton added: "We won the final pretty comfortably against Leicestershire and really it was down to a lovely innings from Fordham, who set the tone from the word go.

"I enjoyed batting with him. We had always got on well, we complemented each other and knew each other's game and what made the other tick.

"There was no professional jealousy and we remain good friends to this day.

"Lamby quite enjoyed the way we both played and complemented each other but we probably took the piss a bit too much for his liking!

"We opened together at times for two or three years and I liked the way Forders would just go for it. He was probably unlucky never to have got a shot at playing for England because he was as prolific and entertaining an opening batsman as anyone around at that time.

"But at that time Keith Fletcher was in charge of the England set up and he never got a chance purely and simply because Fletcher didn't rate him.

"It's not as if he ever scored runs against Essex and it's not as if some more ordinary cricketers from Essex didn't get a chance at international level. But what summed it up for me was a match at Chelmsford in 1990 when Fordham took 159 off the Essex attack with Fletcher watching from the pavilion.

"Forders then holed out going for another big hit and I heard Fletcher say 'one slog too many'."

Coverdale said: "The final against Leicestershire was regarded by many as being a foregone conclusion but we put in a clinical, professional performance to win the match comfortably.

"The fact we were expected to win took nothing away from the joy of winning.

"Too often, as losing finalists, we experienced the low of being dragged out onto the balcony to watch the other team lift the trophy.

"I have never understood why that has to be so. Defeated finalists should not be made to go out.

"I remember the despair after losing to Nottinghamshire in 1987.

"Getting the team out on to the balcony after that was actually one of the hardest things I ever had to do.

"Alan Fordham's was a masterful display and Rob Bailey and Allan Lamb saw us home.

"Tony Lewis summarised the match by saying that Northamptonshire were 'a fine young side, and one who could look to dominate for years to come'.

"Mike Procter was of course moving on, having been approached to take South Africa back into the international cricketing fold. But at the nightclub celebration after the final, he was still in two minds about taking the job.

"He was pretty emotional, for he genuinely felt that the side might dominate English cricket for the next decade.

"However, the South Africa job was a great opportunity for him and one that was too good to turn down.

"Mike was a good man-manager and had won the respect of the players. He brought everyone together and let them play. He did a good job for Northamptonshire cricket.

"Unless you win a major trophy, it means nothing. No-one remembers the runners-up or the gallant losers, they only remember the winners.

"The win put the club on the map and was a great return for the chairman Lynn Wilson who had invested so much of his energies in the quest for success.

"The win allowed the club to move forward, our Centre of Excellence and scouting system leading the way for others to follow.

**175**

"Our stock within cricket rose. We had already established ourselves as a friendly club, where visitors would be guaranteed a warm welcome.

"But now we were also seen as ambitious, a club that made a profit in 15 consecutive years but a club that never lost touch with its supporter 'family' base.

"Lynn Wilson was a wonderful chairman, an incredibly supportive man who opened a number of doors and enabled the club to flourish.

"He never ever betrayed his wealth and I learned so much from him. During my time at Northamptonshire, I was blessed with having the best committee in the country."

A trip to play Leicestershire at Grace Road rounded off the Championship season.

A sporting declaration from the Foxes enabled a Northamptonshire victory and third place in the Championship to go with the NatWest pot – a season where potential had been largely fulfilled, although the title was still proving elusive.

Bailey scored 167 and once again it was Lamb's brilliance that sealed the deal, Northamptonshire winning eight of their 22 Championship matches.


## BRIDGE UNDER THE WATER?

It proved to be a difficult year for captain Allan Lamb in many ways but he ended up lifting a trophy – Lamby was fond of mixing up his sayings and, in his own words, may have been keen to point out that it was all 'bridge under the water now!' And as for the strength of his Northamptonshire side? 'We've got the best paper on team!'

Lamb was eventually fined £6,000 by the Test and County Cricket Board for his Pakistan outburst but the least said about the farcical position adopted by the International Cricket Council throughout the whole issue the better!

The new season of 1993 brought with it much expectation that Northamptonshire would make that quantum leap and land the Championship for the first time.

The debate over blooding young players was still raging although there was understandable reluctance to tamper too much with a side that had begun to acquire a winning mentality.

Bailey said: "There was always a lot of talk about giving young players a chance to establish themselves.

"A case in point was Tony Penberthy, who found himself up against Capes and Kevin Curran for an all-rounder place in the first team.

"Curran played his part in our successes and, in truth, the difference between him and Penberthy was immense.

"Put it this way, if you had to choose two out of three potential match winners from David Capel, Kevin Curran and Tony Penberthy, I think you would have chosen Capes and Curran every time."

With Procter having left for a big new challenge with the returning South Africa, it was decided to replace him with Phil Neale, who had enjoyed much success as captain of a strong Worcestershire team and was looking to step up into management.

Felton said: "After winning the NatWest, we really should have followed that up with the Benson & Hedges Cup in 1993.

"But I remember a long day in the field against Worcestershire prior to our B&H game against Derbyshire in early June.

"We were drained going into the game on what, unusually for Derby, was a baking hot day. We were easily beaten. If we'd have gone into that game in a better state, I think we'd have won and set up a tie with Lancashire in the next round.

"And I reckon we'd have developed the momentum to go all the way. But it wasn't to be.     **177**

"The rest of the season was all a bit negative after that and personally I could see the writing on the wall.

"I'd picked up a couple of man-of-the-match awards but there was a clear push to get Richard Montgomerie, who was near to completing his studies at Oxford, into the first team as opener.

"Phil Neale was a nice enough man, a capable county cricketer who enjoyed considerable success as a captain.

"But in truth we didn't need a manager to replace Procter. He had only come in because Lamby was away quite a bit. Lamby was now fully back in the fold and he and Bob Carter worked well together.

"Phil was really surplus to our needs and he later moved to Warwickshire, and then England.

"Lamby's captaincy had come on leaps and bounds, not least because he was round the club on a full-time basis, and it clicked. All the players got to know Lamby much better at this time and, when I look back now, they were six great years at Northamptonshire.

"I was lucky to be part of a very talented side that benefited from the introduction of the likes of Alan Fordham and Paul Taylor, who gave the side a clear impetus at exactly the right time.

"When you consider why Taylor was brought in, you have to hand it to Bob Carter – he clearly saw something in him to make that move. Northamptonshire represented a second chance for me and a second chance for Taylor, there were quite a few us in that boat."

At Hove against Sussex in the Championship, it was back to the Blaster of old as Bailey hit a blistering double century.

But it was a Northamptonshire old boy who hit the headlines for his new county at Harrogate.

Mark Robinson had moved to his native Yorkshire in 1991 and returned stunning figures of 9-37 against his former county in a rain-affected match at St George's Road.     **178**

At Lord's against Middlesex, Northamptonshire folded to defeat after Curran displayed considerable chutzpah in getting after England spinner Phil Tufnell and getting his decision-making horribly wrong!

Having scored a duck in the first innings, Northamptonshire were batting to stay in the game having been made to follow on.

Curran came to the crease to join skipper Lamb and faced up to Tufnell, who had removed him first time round.

Instead of taking up a circumspect position to the first ball he received, Curran's game plan was to take the fight to Tufnell and aim to put ball one into St John's Wood Road.

Deceived by the flight of the ball, he slogged wildly a third of the way down the pitch and was stumped by a country mile?! Tufnell clearly saw him coming!

Lamb's response at the non-striker's end said it all as he threw his bat onto the floor and stared icily into space as Curran turned back to the pavilion.

The clear need to stabilise the innings and build a recovery had foundered on the back of one very rash stroke.

The second innings thereafter ebbed away and Northamptonshire went down by ten wickets.

Curran took some ribbing, from players and spectators alike, and it was Coverdale, some while later writing in the club's annual end-of-season report, who sought to defend Curran's actions.

Coverdale claimed that although the plan did not come off, it remained a valid plan. In my view, the plan should not have been given any validity in the first place. We'll have to agree to disagree on that one!

History was made towards the end of a disappointing summer when Northamptonshire claimed their first-ever one-day victory over Lancashire at Old Trafford.

Ripley said: "Old Trafford is not my favourite ground, especially as someone who was born the other side of the Pennines.

**179**

"We had a bad record up there and went up for the game the day before. The forecast for the day of the match was dire so, with the prospect of little play, we had a few drinks the night before.

"The forecast didn't pan out, the match was played and Curtly Ambrose, who'd had a few Baileys the night before, had to be talked into playing And when he got out there he appeared to be running backwards, such was his enthusiasm!

"He complained all day that he had the flu, when everyone else clearly knew it was a hangover!"

Capel added: "It was good for us to get that win at Old Trafford and it kept one old man quiet on this occasion.

"The man in question always used to open the little gate as you came down on to the field from the pavilion.

"His greeting never changed: 'Nice to see you Mr Capel, don't be long out there.' And more often than not I wasn't!"

Off the field, Northamptonshire's bedfellows Northampton Town Football Club were set to move to a new home of their own in the west of the town.

But, as Coverdale explained, the move away from the cricket ground was far from straightforward.

He said: "Northampton Town were due to move out to a new home, the Sixfields Stadium, provided by the local borough council.

"But it wasn't a smooth process and, at one stage, both club chairman Lynn Wilson and myself had severe doubts that they would ever move out at all.

"So much so, that Lynn and I took a great deal of time out to look around Northampton for a possible new home for the cricket club. We looked at a number of potential sites, notably one at Delapre Abbey.

"We even went as far as drawing up some reasonably detailed plans and discussing with the Test and County Cricket Board the possibility of housing a new national Academy as part of this complex, something that their then chairman, Dennis Silk, was very keen to consider. **180**

"He personally was very excited by the idea. However the Academy idea was not really supported by the TCCB at that time. And Northampton Town finally did make the move to Sixfields late in 1994.

"We still had the bowls club to provide for as part of the Cockerill Trust agreement and their future move away from the County Ground would prove to be equally awkward!"

If 1993 was disappointing, a distinct lack of an upturn in fortunes the following year was depressing. The campaign got off to the worst possible start when Ambrose once again went absent without leave.

Ambrose had been playing for the West Indies against England in the Caribbean series dominated by that magnificent batsman Brian Lara who had hit an unbeaten Test 400 in Antigua. Accordingly he was tired at the end of another long series and decided to take an extended break.

He was expected to have returned to Northampton in time for the Benson & Hedges Cup preliminary round tie with Middlesex at Lord's on 26 April. But the game came around, there was no sign of Ambrose, Northamptonshire were dumped out of the competition and a furious Lamb vented his spleen at a press conference.

From that late April Cup exit, the season ignominiously fizzled out. It was to be my last season on the circuit and it was great to see Brian Lara in his pomp, hitting 197 for Warwickshire in a Championship win at Northampton.

My last away trip was to Southampton, the highlight being a night out at the Concord Club in Eastleigh.

Somehow, an enterprising band of Northamptonshire supporters had somehow talked their way into the establishment claiming to be part of Hampshire skipper Mark Nicholas' party!

And a late-season Sunday game against Essex at Chelmsford introduced a confident 16-year-old by the name of David Sales, who walked to the crease with a swagger and proceeded to take a half century off the home attack.          **181**

It's a sight that has never left me – Sales had all the attributes of a fantastic batsman but things didn't quite work out for him and he also never got to represent his country on the biggest stage.

Coverdale summed up: "There was an expectation that we would be one of the dominant teams in the years following our NatWest success.

"We should have been, there was a disappointment that we weren't.

"At times we were average at best. Some of our younger players were beginning to get a taste of first-team cricket and I think Lamby expected Curtly to roll over teams.

"But other sides adapted their game plans to make sure they saw Curtly off and then maybe get on top of other bowlers in our attack.

"We didn't make any real impression in the Championship, or in any of the cup competitions, but a change in overseas player for 1995 changed our outlook."

Coverdale also reflected on Phil Neale's unsuccessful spell at Wantage Road.

He added: "Phil seemed to tick all the boxes for us above any other candidate as a replacement for Mike Procter. He came into the role straight from the dressing room, and he was an arch professional.

"But frankly when he had been the captain of Worcestershire he hadn't been too popular with our players and staff and in retrospect it was the wrong appointment.

"Lamby was no longer in the England frame and so spent more time at the club. He was proving to be an inspirational captain and he no longer required the level of support that Mike Procter had given when he wasn't around, playing for England.

"It was never quite clear who was in charge, Phil or Lamby, and it just didn't work out.

"Eventually, at the end of the 1994 season, Dennis Amiss made an approach for Phil to join Warwickshire. **182**

"We agreed to release him from his contract and he met with a lot of success at Edgbaston. The time just wasn't right for him at Northamptonshire."

## KEEP ATTACKING!

Allan Lamb, with assistance from Bob Carter, took over the Northamptonshire ship in 1995... and what a superlative year it turned out to be in many respects.

The disappointments of 1993 and 1994 were soon cast asunder as Lamb led the team astutely on an attacking crusade which had the rest of the country sitting up and taking notice.

Some of the matches were jaw-droppingly exciting and, for so long, it looked like this would be the year where everything finally came together in a manner which would realise every Tudor Rose follower's wildest dreams.

The Championship was within reach - as it turned, it didn't come together that way.   But no matter, this was a stunning summer of cricket at Wantage Road and one which anyone who witnessed some of those matches will ever forget.

Capel was back in the fold having been laid low with a myriad of injuries, notably a broken arm and a floating bone in the knee joint, during his Benefit Year.

He said: "1995 was a special season for everyone involved and I was pleased to make a contribution to what was a magnificent team effort during that year. I wanted to repay the Northamptonshire public, my Benefit committee and the lads at the club for their incredible generosity.

"Allan Lamb captained the side particularly well during 1995 and one of our key players during the season was Anil Kumble, who took 110 wickets and bowled more than 1,000 overs.

"He would invariably bowl from the difficult end for seamers as a stock bowler.                                    **183**

"This enabled the seamers to stay fresh and perform physically and mentally at their peak and, as a unit, we found ourselves bowling sides out twice.

"Allan Lamb and Bob Carter complemented each other well – Carter was a good foil, a great club man.

"I enjoyed fielding in the slips alongside Allan Lamb and Kevin Curran, who had a very good cricket brain. There was a very good synergy between us out there."

Coverdale said: "We noticed that Anil Kumble might be available as an overseas player but there didn't seem to be any much interest in him. Lamby rang Mohammad Azharuddin to get his number and sound him out and, with Curtly Ambrose on tour with the West Indies, Anil agreed to come over.

"His first introduction to county cricket was a Sunday League match at Derby where we got slaughtered.

"Frankly Anil did not look great on that occasion. But I remember Rob Bailey coming over to me a few days later after batting against him in the nets and saying 'what a fantastic bowler this guy is'. He just loved to bowl and sent the ball down at a fair pace but with a dip and unerring accuracy and would bowl or trap a lot who played back to him.

"Anil would keep it tight for long periods from one end, allowing the others to bowl in short, sharp spells of four, five or six overs."

The Northamptonshire side had a settled look about it in 1995 and there were some key factors that accounted for a tremendous summer of cricket.

At the top of the order, Fordham and Bailey were given licence to attack.

Kevin Curran and David Capel, down at seven, delivered powerful support.

Neil Mallender and Paul Taylor provided the spearhead but Anil Kumble was the ace in the pack and ultimately made the difference.

Here are ten Northamptonshire games in a 'roll of honour' from the Championship season that summer.     **184**

BANGALORE, Karnataka, India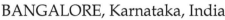
ANIL KUMBLE
Born: 17 October 1970
Northamptonshire: 1995
Nickname: Apple
RHB/LB

**27 April v Kent at Canterbury**
**Northamptonshire: 561 (Richard Montgomerie 192, David Capel 167)**
**Kent: 352**
**Kent: 215 (Paul Taylor 5-49)**
**Northamptonshire: 7-1**
**Northamptonshire won by 9 wickets**
**Comment: Richard Montgomerie batted for ten hours and he and David Capel established a high-scoring fourth-wicket partnership.**

18 May v Surrey at Northampton
Northamptonshire: 403 (Allan Lamb 166, Kevin Curran 117)
Surrey: 263
Northamptonshire: 59
Surrey: 190
Northamptonshire won by 9 runs
Comment: A second innings score of 59 however raised huge doubts about securing the win bonus but Surrey were then skittled out ten runs short of victory in a tense final chapter!
A tremendous match which set the stall out for the rest of the season – Northamptonshire actually scored the highest and the two lowest scores of the 1995 campaign... and ended up winning all three matches in which the scores were registered! **185**

25 May v Yorkshire at Sheffield
Yorkshire: 250
Northamptonshire: 357 (Rob Bailey 111)
Yorkshire: 252
Northamptonshire: 146-3
Northamptonshire won by 7 wickets
Comment: Covered this match for the Sunday Times and it was my first good luck at Anil Kumble who weaved his magic around the Tykes batsmen – especially the hapless Richard Blakey, whom Kumble knew how to wrap around his spinning finger!

15 June v Essex at Luton
Essex: 127 (David Capel 5-29)
Northamptonshire: 46 (Mark Ilott 9-19)
Essex: 107 (Paul Taylor 7-50)
Northamptonshire: 192-8 (Allan Lamb 50no)
Northamptonshire won by 2 wickets
Comment: For nerve-shattering drama, this match topped even the Surrey cliffhanger.
The sides met on a Luton track that traditionally favoured the batsmen.
But would this time round it would prove to be a haven for the swing bowlers, especially the left-armers in the pack.
Capel put the skids under Essex in the first innings of the match only for Northamptonshire to fold for just 46 – a first-innings deficit of 81, Mark Ilott claiming nine wickets.
Ilott's England rival Paul Taylor then snapped back, bagging seven wickets as Essex were bowled out for 107, a lead of 188.
Could Northamptonshire make the highest score of the match and get there?
Well they did, just, thanks to an unbeaten fifty from the man for the moment, Allan Lamb.          **186**

Coverdale said: "The summer of 1995 was a very good one weather wise and the team was involved in some tremendous games of cricket.

"Phil Neale had moved on and Lamby was in sole charge.

"Anil Kumble had replaced Curtly Ambrose as the overseas player and Russell Warren was in the side ahead of David Ripley.

"It was felt that Russell would play as a keeper and give us more depth to our batting.

"David Ripley was the better wicketkeeper but in fairness Russell didn't miss much that season and kept to a pretty high standard.

"There was a great victory against Surrey in May, when we were bowled out for 59 in our second innings and then got them out for 190. It provided tremendous entertainment.

"And there was also an incredible match at Luton, normally a great batting track.

"It was over in two days and saw 28 wickets go down on day one.

"Essex were out for 127, we were then out for 46 but somehow we managed to get them out cheaply again for 107.

"This set us 189 to win in the final innings, an improbable target in light of what had gone before, but we really got stuck in and got there with two wickets to spare.

"Anil won that game for us with his batting on this occasion!

"It was a game for the swing bowlers with David Capel among the wickets in the Essex first innings to set the ball rolling.

"Paul Taylor got 7-50 in their second but Mark Ilott took 14 wickets in the match, including an amazing 9-19 in our score of 46."

**22 June v Leicestershire at Northampton**
**Northamptonshire: 564 (David Capel 175)**
**Leicestershire: 367**
**Leicestershire: 160**
**Northamptonshire won by an innings and 37 runs**
**Comment: Northamptonshire out batted their local foes in the first innings, David Capel, batting at seven, scoring a career-best 175 in an innings victory.**

20 July v Hampshire at Northampton
Hampshire: 560 (Anil Kumble 7-131)
Northamptonshire: 321
Northamptonshire: 365 (Alan Fordham 120)
Hampshire: 118-8 (Anil Kumble 6-61)
Match drawn
Comment: Anil Kumble took seven wickets but visitors Hampshire racked up a formidable first-innings total. Northamptonshire were asked to follow on, but a fine century put considerable pressure on Hampshire to win a game they had always seemed confident of winning. Kumble, 13 wickets in the match, turned the screw in the last innings and both teams got close to the finishing line in a tense finale.

Coverdale said: "The belief in the side grew as the campaign.

"This was amply demonstrated when Hampshire came to Northampton and took an early stranglehold on the match.

"They scored 560 well into the second day and were crowing.

"This intensified when they bowled us out for 321 to enforce the follow-on.

"But second time round we scored 365 and, needing 127 to win, they were left hanging on at 118-8 in the final session. **188**

27 July v Warwickshire at Edgbaston
Northamptonshire: 152
Warwickshire: 224 (David Capel 7-44)
Northamptonshire: 346 (Alan Fordham 101)
Warwickshire: 267 (Anil Kumble 7-82)
Northamptonshire won by 7 runs
Comment: A cracking four-day match, David Capel and Anil Kumble starring with the ball and Alan Fordham with the bat as Northamptonshire won a riveting top-of-the-table clash by the narrow margin of seven runs.

Capel said: "It was an incredible game to be involved in. I do remember at lunch on the final day that Dermot Reeve had gone up to the table and eaten the vegetarian options, effectively depriving Anil Kumble of any lunch.

"All Anil said was 'don't worry Capes, I'll be having three Bears after lunch'. This performance from Anil Kumble was a highlight of the season, to take seven wickets in such a high-pressure game.

"He was as good as his word, dismissing Dermot Reeve and ending the innings with match-winning figures. Lamby said it was the best four-day game he'd taken part in.

"It was a terrific contest between two top teams really knocking it out of each other. For them, Allan Donald bowled brilliantly and Tim Munton also performed very well – I always admired Munton's effort and tenacity on a pitch that had flattened out.

"Alan Fordham scored a ton in our second innings, a very good knock, and it was all out attack in the fourth innings with Anil leading us forward.

"When they required 30 runs or so to win, I asked to go on to bowl and actually bowled a bit wide of the crease to Munton as they closed in to the target.

"I got one to angle in to him, Ken Palmer upheld the lbw appeal and we'd won an incredible game."     189

3 August v Durham at Northampton
Durham: 148 (Anil Kumble 5-26)
Northamptonshire: 492-5dec (Rob Bailey 132)
Durham: 268 (Wayne Larkins 112)
Northamptonshire won by an innings and 76 runs
Comment: A comfortable victory for Northamptonshire after Rob Bailey had piloted the side into a commanding first innings position.
A century for Wayne Larkins against his old county proved to be in vain.

**10 August v Gloucestershire at Northampton**
**Northamptonshire: 321**
**Gloucestershire: 293 (Anil Kumble 6-76)**
**Northamptonshire: 312**
**Gloucestershire: 131**
**Northamptonshire won by 209 runs**
**Comment: Northamptonshire were always a step ahead in this match, relying once again on the guile of Anil Kumble to turn the screw.**

24 August v Nottinghamshire at Northampton
Nottinghamshire: 527
Northamptonshire: 781-7dec (Russell Warren 154, Alan Fordham 130, Allan Lamb 115, David Capel 114no)
Nottinghamshire: 157 (Anil Kumble 5-43)
Northamptonshire won by an innings and 97 runs
Comment: An incredible match as Nottinghamshire, like Hampshire before them, posted more than 500 on the board in the first innings.
But Lamb was not fazed, ordering his troops to bat the opposition into submission and this they did by replying with 781 – the highest total by anyone in 1995 - including no less than four different century-makers.
It proved too much for Nottinghamshire, who slipped to an innings defeat, Kumble again doing the damage.   **190**

Coverdale said: "We beat the eventual champions Warwickshire at Edgbaston in a fantastic game of four-day cricket, one of the best ever matches in the competition in the opinion of many who played in or watched the game.

"And towards the end of the season we beat Nottinghamshire at Northampton and this after they had scored 527 in the first innings of the match.

"We responded with a mammoth 781-7 declared which batted them into submission and then dismissed them for 157 to win by an innings.

"The following game was away against fellow title rivals Middlesex at Uxbridge, which ended in a draw, a result which only suited Warwickshire. The pitch was far too good to get a result."

## TRICKY ABOUT DICKIE

The Middlesex draw preceded the trip to Lord's for a battle royale against Warwickshire in the final of the NatWest Trophy.

Capel said: "Anil again bowled very well for us in this final and Dermot Reeve survived a loud appeal on a straight one from Anil to go on and win the match for Warwickshire."

Coverdale added: "We had got to Lord's by beating Yorkshire at Headingley in the semis, a result that gave me a great deal of personal satisfaction. It was one of the best performances by the team in all my years at Northampton.

"We had gone up there seemingly as sacrificial lambs as far as the Yorkshire fans were concerned and were playing to a full house, with the Western Terrace heaving and in good voice from early in the day.

"Rob Bailey scored an unbeaten 93 to help us to a big score which proved too much for Yorkshire.        **191**

"We weren't on top of our game at Lord's but, to this day, I cannot account for umpire Dickie Bird's decision not to give out Dermot Reeve when he was plum lbw to Anil Kumble.

"It was one of the most embarrassing moments that anyone involved in cricket could ever remember.

"When the replay came up on TV there was total silence from the commentators.

"That itself spoke volumes!

"Reeve was on four at the time and went on to win the match for Warwickshire and seal the championship and trophy double.

"We all knew that if Reeve had been given out we would have gone on to win the match.

"But most of all it was a real crying shame to miss out on winning our first-ever championship.

"In any other year, the amount of Championship wins we achieved in 1995 would have been enough for us to win the title.

"But we eventually finished third behind Middlesex who, like us, had won 12 matches while Warwickshire had managed to win 14.

"So again it was a cruel summer in that we came away empty-handed but there was some magnificent entertainment along the way."

Bailey summed up: "We had some good times in the early 1990s when we played some excellent cricket but they were also frustrating times as we never got to shake off our 'nearly men' tag.

"Even in 1987 we lost the two domestic Cup finals and I know Geoff Cook to this day still struggles to come to terms with it.

"But we can look back on some great games and providing great memories for a lot of people associated with the club and those outside the county borders who enjoyed our attacking style. **192**

"We had a very strong dressing room filled with some very good cricketers and tough characters and this had much to do with the success we enjoyed.

"The 1995 season was incredible and we were involved in many fantastic games of cricket.

"We beat Warwickshire in a fabulous four-day game at Edgbaston and Capes played a massive part in this match.

"I was fielding at slip when he had last man Tim Munton lbw to give us a thrilling victory."

Ripley had mixed feelings about the season as he had been kept out of the first team by Russell Warren.

He said: "It was a great year for the first team but I wasn't part of that.

"I was scoring runs in second team cricket but I'd lost my first team place to Russell Warren, who was picked for batting and wicket keeping to allow for another bowler in the eleven.

"That season we had Anil Kumble, a slow bowler who sent down good-paced deliveries with deadly accuracy.

"The slip needed to be a long way back for Anil and it was a good test for a wicket keeper.

"I felt I would have kept wicket better to Anil than Russell did.

"But the results were good, the team was winning and on that basis it was a good year to be around."

A smashing summer of cricket proved to the last hurrah for captain Allan Lamb who made a snap decision to stand down before the start of the 1996 season.

It was truly the end of an era, with Lamb quitting the club to concentrate on a second Benefit and a new book launch.

Coverdale said: "During the closed season, chairman Lynn Wilson and I were aware that there were problems ahead with Lamby's determination to go into print with a book which was bound to focus on the ball tampering row on the back of the previous Pakistan tour.

*Rob Bailey and Allan Lamb batting at Derby*
*– Bailey took over the captaincy from Lamb in 1996*

"A lot of meetings took place behind the scenes around the Test and County Cricket Board regulations at the time which stated that a cricketer who was active in the game could not have a book published without it being vetted and approved by the TCCB. **194**

"Discussions with the TCCB hierarchy did not prove successful and solicitor Brent Hill was hired as a 'problem solver' in an attempt to find a way forward which would keep Lamby under contract with us and enable him to go into print.

"But it would come down to the TCCB asking Lamby to sign an undertaking that he would not publish the book without it being approved.

"Lamby felt he couldn't sign the undertaking as he wanted the book to go ahead unchanged but of course this meant he could no longer remain a Northamptonshire cricketer.

"I don't think it was a decision he took lightly. He went to see the players off on their pre-season tour a few days later and he appeared gutted to be out of it.

"At the end of one of the many meetings which we held, I remember Brent advising Lamby strongly against taking on Imran Khan in a libel action.

"But Lamby and Ian Botham went ahead with it and it resulted in a very costly defeat for them."

Anil Kumble was no longer in the fold, Bob Carter too had returned to New Zealand and John Emburey, who had been tapped up at Uxbridge the previous season, came in as director of cricket and was clearly still keen to turn his arm over out in the middle.

Rob Bailey took over as captain from Lamb and forged a working partnership with Emburey which resulted in Northamptonshire reaching the final of the Benson and Hedges Cup against Lancashire, although they were routinely beaten at Lord's.

Capel had been given a pinch-hitting role in the one-day side and enjoyed the role.

He said: "Rob was very supportive and there was a good transition of younger players taking more prominent roles in the Championship game.

Bailey said: "The powerplays were introduced in the 1990s and Capes was the ideal man for such a situation.     **195**

*Curtly Ambrose and Kevin Curran walk from the nets at Lord's prior to the 1996 Benson and Hedges Cup Final against Lancashire*

-----------------------------------------------------------------

"A lot of batsmen then needed time to play themselves in but powerplays needed someone with the ability to get going from ball one.

"Capes had that ability and, certainly in that respect, was slightly ahead of his time. **196**

"It's a shame he never got play in the Twenty20 competitions.

"I think he would have been very good at it, modern limited-overs cricket is ideally suited to his game."

One of the younger players really beginning to stamp his mark on the team was the confident Sales.

He had people sitting up and taking notice with a debut double century in a Championship game with Worcestershire at Kidderminster.

Capel said: "He got a duck in the first innings for David Sales and nearly picked up a pair in the second innings, on a good deck, when Vikram Solanki got one to turn out of Paul Taylor's footmarks.

"Salesy got an inside nick on to his belly and the ball dropped just short of silly point.

"I was batting at the other end and he convinced me that if he'd had a washboard stomach he'd have been out, the paunch had softened the blow!

"He soon got into his stride with a fierce drive and shouted 'I'm away'.

"He started hitting some beautiful shots and I suddenly noticed that he'd overtaken me, not least when he said to me 'come on, catch up!' He was a very confident young cricketer."

Sales was quick to pay tribute to Capel, whom he regarded as a mentor throughout his career at Wantage Road.

He said: "My outstanding memory of a performance by David was when he opened the batting at the Oval for Northants against Surrey in a 40-over game and smashed their international bowling line-up to all parts of the ground.

"He went on to score a magnificent century. The reason that this stood out for me was just the sheer clean hitting and stroke play, it was brilliant.

"But the word 'intense' and David Capel go together. I feel if he did not have this he would not have achieved what he did.

**197**

CARSHALTON, Surrey, England
DAVID SALES
Born: 3 December 1977
Northamptonshire: 1994 to present
Nickname: Jumble
RHB/RM

*David Sales hits out in a game against*
*Worcestershire, on the receiving end of a*
*double century on Jumble's first-class*
*debut at Kidderminster in 1996*

**198**

"Intensity can be lots of different things and, in his character, intensity was a major factor in his success, along with the passion and dedication he put in.

"David was a magnificent all-rounder, we were very fortunate at Northampton to have him batting at five and either opening the bowling, or first change.

"It really did make a difference having himself and Kevin Curran in the same side as both were quality all-rounders.

"David's batting was always positive and his bowling always aggressive, that is why he was such a great asset."

At the end of 1996, Curtly Ambrose ended his association with Northamptonshire – Tony Penberthy was now established in the middle order and a precocious young off-spinner going by the name of Graeme Swann was beginning to come into the reckoning.

Coverdale reflected: "Rob Bailey was appointed captain and John Emburey came in as director of cricket on a four-year contract. Soon he ended up playing for us.

"We reached another domestic final, the Benson & Hedges Cup, after an epic semi-final win against Warwickshire at the County Ground.

"Tim Walton hit the headlines in that game with his prowess in the field and I recall sitting in my office with the third umpire Barrie Leadbeater, a very good friend of mine, as the decisions had to be made by him.

"Barrie had to adjudicate decisions using a small television screen with a very fuzzy reception.

"He had a few run outs to call and I'm baffled as to how he was able to give any decision with any great degree of certainty!

"We were well beaten in the final against Lancashire. Curtly struggled with a leg injury and Paul Taylor experienced a touch of 'the yips'.

"Capes had done very well as a pinch-hitter in the competition but unfortunately got a duck in the final.    **199**

"And it was the end of an era as this was to be Curtly Ambrose's last season with the club."

Bailey could not look back on the 1997 season, his last as skipper, with any degree of pleasure or satisfaction.

He said: "The 1995 season was a wonderful summer, even though we once again retained the tag as 'nearly men'.

"It got difficult at the end of that year. Allan Lamb decided to quit before the start of the 1996 season and we also lost Anil Kumble, who had taken 100 wickets for us.

"We had lost two major players and I was invited to take on the captaincy which was a challenge I relished.

"Curtly Ambrose came back for a final season in 1996, which was good, and we got to a final.

"Then John Emburey arrived at the club and Kevin Curran was pressing his claims for a more prominent role in team affairs following Lamby's departure.

"We were looking to get younger players more established in the first team, so I couldn't guarantee Capes regular first-team cricket.

"The old order was changing, but it wasn't easy. Russell Warren looked as if he might establish himself as a wicketkeeper/batsman.

Mohammed Akram came in to replace Curtly Ambrose, which was not so good, and the 1997 season was a disaster."

Capel chose to stick with Northamptonshire in spite of being told his first-team opportunities would be increasingly limited.

Bailey added: "I don't know if Capes regrets not moving to another county when he had a chance to do so.

"I left Northamptonshire to play for Derbyshire and it gave me a new lease of life.

"I know he had offers but he turned them down. In the end he took up coaching and management opportunities at Wantage Road.

"But from a playing perspective, I do think it would have done him the world of good." **200**

Coverdale said: "Prior to the start of the season we encouraged John Emburey to start planning for the long term, for the Northamptonshire team of 2000 and several years beyond.

"I think that John took that too literally and changed things too quickly.

"He brought in a number of young players who were probably not quite ready, to the extent that the senior players felt excluded.

"Our overseas player was Mohammad Akram and in truth it wasn't the best signing.

"But he was highly recommended by many respected people in the game.

"We did our homework and spoke to a lot of people before he was signed.

"They all reckoned that he was a fine young bowler who was going to be a real star in the future.

"I remember bringing him to Northampton and settling him in and asking him the following day how things were going.

"He said everything was fine and that he'd gone out for a meal on his first night in Northampton.

"I was happy to hear that and asked him where he'd gone to eat. 'Bradford', came the reply.

"Everyone quickly lost patience with him. In the Benson & Hedges Cup quarter-final against Yorkshire at Headingley, Capes bowled well to win us the game.

"Akram didn't bowl too badly but in the semi-final at Kent he couldn't play because of a facial infection and that match was lost.

"At the end of the season, my PA went to the house where he was staying in Northampton to carry out an inventory.

"It appeared quite a few people had been stopping at the house and what confronted her as she did her checks was pretty disgusting."

NORTHAMPTON, England
MAL LOYE
Born: 27 September 1972
Northamptonshire: 1991 to 2002, 2010 to 2011
RHB/OB

"Alan Fordham, the team vice-captain, retired at the end of the season to take up a position with the English Cricket Board.

"And skipper Rob Bailey stepped down from the captaincy before the 1998 season with Curran, who had an eye on a Benefit Year, installed as the new captain.

It was little short of a disaster, the side under-performing on the field and Curran floundering in his role as captain, strategist and motivator.

One bright light was the partnership of 401 – which remains a Northamptonshire record – between Mal Loye and David Ripley against Glamorgan at Wantage Road early in the season.

Even this did not get the headlines it merited, wiped from the back page by Northampton Town's Wembley play-off final exploits against Grimsby Town on a sunny May afternoon.

Coverdale said: "Devon Malcolm joined up with this season.

"With Rob Bailey stepping down and Alan Fordham retiring, Kevin Curran was the obvious candidate to take over the captaincy.

"But having said that, I think everyone knew full well that with Kevin in charge it would be something of a rollercoaster ride.

"David Capel was coming to the end of the road and while Paul Taylor was still there he also wasn't at the height of his powers. **202**

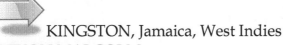

KINGSTON, Jamaica, West Indies
DEVON MALCOLM
Born: 22 February 1963
Northamptonshire: 1998 to 2000
RHB/RF

*Devon Malcolm flanked by team-mates Matthew Hayden and Mal Loye*

-------------------------------------------------------------------

"We'd lined up Paul Reiffel as our overseas player but he pulled out not long before the season was due to start and Kevin Curran, at the eleventh hour, suggested we consider looking at Andy Flower.

"But Kevin was over-ruled as it was felt that we needed a fast bowler and we called upon Franklyn Rose, although he flattered to deceive.

"This was also Kevin's Benefit year but it soon became quite clear that things weren't working out.

"One of the problems was that we had a very strong second team that ended up by winning both the Second Eleven Championship and the one-day competition.

And a group of players all of whom thought they should be playing for the first team. That created a lot of dissatisfaction.

"Symptomatic of the state that matters had reached, near the end of the season the first team were at Bristol at the same time as the Second XI were playing Gloucestershire at the County Ground.

"The home team dressing room was right next to my office and every so often I could make out cheers coming from the dressing room although nothing was actually happening out on the field in front of me.

"When I went in to investigate I found that the second team players were actually cheering the loss of first team wickets at Bristol.

"We had a camp full of frustrated players and that was the end of the road for Kevin, after one year as captain, and for John Emburey too."

This was Capel's last season as a player, unceremoniously cut adrift a month or so before the end of the season courtesy of a brief press statement which did not reflect the huge contribution he had made to Northamptonshire cricket.

The public relations were appalling, notwithstanding the turmoil within the camp this should have been handled so much better that it was.

Capel would have preferred to have bowed out while still playing and being given the chance to thank the crowd one last time. He said: "I didn't get the opportunity to do this as Curran and Penberthy were preferred as the two all-rounders and that was a policy decision."

Bailey added: "At the start of the season the captaincy was up for grabs and I'm sure Capes would have liked to have skippered his home county.                    **204**

"But I think it was important that he focussed entirely upon his own game without needing to really worry about how others were doing, deciding bowling changes and the rest of it.

"His playing role at the club came to an abrupt end towards the end of 1998.

"It was a shame that he didn't get a last hurrah but there is little room for sentiment in the game these days. It is a different game."

So Capel left the arena after 18 years as a player, during which time he scored 12,202 first-class runs for Northamptonshire at an average of 29.68, with a highest score of 175 in 1995.

As a bowler, he took 546 wickets at an average of 32.18, his best bowling figures also coming in that golden year of 1995, 7-44 in that tremendous victory over Warwickshire at Edgbaston.

I felt that the club had let down a player who – as a home-grown cricketer over the best part of two decades – had given heart and soul for the cause.

I wrote in the Chronicle & Echo: 'Capel played heart and soul for Northamptonshire, a cricketer who deserved much better.

'The way this has been done has been a humiliation for Capel, what sort of a message has that sent out?'

Little matter, Capel was retired and Emburey and Curran also moved on at the end of the season, the much-vaunted 21st century blueprint not worth the paper it was written on.

But at least Capel was not permanently cast adrift – his coaching expertise proved a more than useful asset and he was taken on to manage the emerging Academy programme in 1999 as the club's first director of excellence.

Bailey said: "David went straight from quitting playing into the development job with the club, so in that respect things worked out well for him.

**205**

"I respected the fact that he started out at the bottom in coaching and put in the time to get himself to the top and where he needed to be. He didn't go straight into the top job as some people do.

"Capes has always had a passion for coaching and some of the time during the off season we would coach together.

"He has coached throughout his career and, typically, he has done it with a passion. He had always wanted to do it and achieved his ambition."

Sales said: "His county cricket career was very good, he was a star performer with bat and ball for Northamptonshire who would never give up. He did very well to play international cricket, it was just a shame it was in the same era as Botham otherwise, I feel, he would have played a lot more.

"When David first went into the coaching side, we did a lot of batting together and I used his knowledge of the game, and of my game in particular, to help me progress.

"He has always been a very passionate man and he knows his cricket inside out. He's always trying to help people improve themselves and is technically very good at finding ways that you can improve."

Coverdale admitted that the move to Academy status was not without its troubles, notably the political wrangling between the bodies who had traditionally entrenched vested interests in promoting youth cricket in Northamptonshire.

Coverdale said: "We were one of the first four counties to be given Academy status and we were indebted to coach Bob Carter, who had returned to the club in 1999, and fitness guru Richard Smith in getting that recognition. We were in fact the only non-Test match ground to be recognised, it was a great feather in our cap.

"It enabled us to bring in former Essex paceman Neil Foster to get the wheels in motion and while we were always on the lookout for local talent, we didn't let up on our scouting network. **206**

*Steve Coverdale chats with Michael Vaughan – the former England skipper was looked at by Northamptonshire*

"Brian Reynolds had become our Cricket Development Officer way back in 1986 and we had scouts in all parts of the country, predominantly in Cornwall, Staffordshire and also in Durham, Lancashire and Yorkshire where the league set-ups are very strong.

"We deliberately decided to avoid the south-east, where there already so many counties but even then, frankly, I don't think that there was a promising young cricketer in the country who didn't come on to our radar.

"Our recruitment policy was aggressive and we sailed close to the wind on some occasions.

Michael Vaughan and Matthew Hoggard were sent down to us to attend our Centre of Excellence sessions.

"We trailed Andrew Flintoff quite keenly for some time and, in previous years, we'd also had the chance to bring in the likes of Kim Barnett, Tim Robinson and Richard Illingworth.

"You could put together a pretty good side of players who we looked at and for one reason or another we didn't eventually sign.

"Many years earlier my predecessor Ken Turner had West Indies opener Gordon Greenidge down for a trial at Northampton.

"Ken apparently didn't rate him and advised him forget about cricket and told him to "stick to driving a bus'.

"Unsurprisingly, Gordon went on to score quite a few runs against Northamptonshire!

"Apart from allowing us to look at youngsters from around the country, the Centre of Excellence's main aim was to improve the standard of local cricketers and positively nurture home-grown talent.

"Before that, the county cricket club had always experienced something of an uneasy relationship with the two bodies responsible for promoting young cricketers in the county, the Northamptonshire Cricket Association and the Northamptonshire Schools Cricket Association. **208**

"The NCA seemed to be a little empire in itself, run by extremely well-meaning individuals but many of them wanting a slice of kudos and glory.

"They had a very fixed approach to coaching youngsters. My ten-year-old son Paul was often bowled into the ground at afternoon coaching sessions run by the NCA. It wasn't the best way to bring on young cricketers.

"The Association was run by John Malfait, a popular local figure who had a firm view about the way cricket should be run in the county.

"John and his colleagues often presented a problem when anyone presented a different view.

"But when the English Cricket Board was on the verge of bringing in county boards, we had to be quite firm with the NCA and tell them that this was the new way forward and there was no alternative. Individually they were very welcome to join this new venture which one or two did, but things were going to be done differently.

"The Schools' set-up, run by John Wake, also came on board and thankfully the politics of vested interests are now a thing of the distant past.

"Alan Hodgson did a great deal of good in finding a way forward for all parties, especially with the various leagues and clubs in the county, but it was a very long process."


## WORLD CUP FIX AT WANTAGE ROAD

Steve Coverdale also had his hands full with the 1999 Cricket World Cup in England, which was bringing two group matches to Wantage Road in May.

He said: "We were granted two matches and also hosted the Sri Lanka team, then the reigning world champions.

"One of the matches was that between Sri Lanka and South Africa, one of the major matches in the first phase of the competition. It was a real coup for the club.      **209**

"Preparations for the World Cup had started nearly three years earlier.

"Plans for staging the matches were based around our new Indoor Cricket Centre, which had been built on the old football ground at the northern end of the ground.

"We had to actually construct the facility, which meant working throughout the 1998 season which was a challenge in itself.

"Our World Cup preparations were thoroughly scrutinised throughout by Michael Browning, an Australian who had run the Commonwealth Games in Brisbane, who was in charge of the whole competition.

"He told me later that he initially thought that we would never be able to stage a World Cup match at Wantage Road but, after completing the competition, he said that Northampton was one of the best-prepared venues, a great accolade for everyone who played a part in getting us ready.

"Former police inspector Trevor Finch made sure we were prepared for every eventuality.

"Prior to the two games, early in 1999, we held a desktop exercise at the ground where we were tested how we would deal with a number of major incident scenarios in real time.

"That lasted a whole day and a lot of people thought this level of preparation was a little bit over the top.

"But while you hope everything goes smoothly on the day, and usually it does, for us it didn't and we ended up being very grateful to Trevor and his exercise!

"For the game between Sri Lanka and South Africa, we had a small demonstration at the ground, a death in the indoor school stand and a plane flying a banner above the ground.

"All these incidents tested our emergency response and the police certainly moved in on the banner-flying pilot in double quick time! The South African cricketers didn't play ball either, choosing to indulge in a six-hitting competition as part of their warm-up. **210**

"Cricket balls were flying everywhere, risking damage and personal safety, and in the end I had to have strong words with the captain, Hansie Cronje, asking him to stop. It was both stupid and childish.

"In the Pakistan and Bangladesh tie, we had people running through back gardens of nearby houses and scaling walls to get into the ground.

"The match was a sell-out but I suspect there were several thousand more in the ground than had actually bought tickets!

"Bangladesh against all the odds won and that match, of course, hit the headlines in the years to come for all the wrong reasons, this time it was Pakistan and allegations of match-fixing."

As for the domestic campaign, 1999 was a little bit of a stepping stone building towards big hopes for the new Millennium.

Coverdale added: "Everyone seemed to agree with my suggestion that we should approach the Australian Matthew Hayden as overseas player and captain.

"I flew Down Under to finalise the details for Bob's return, met with Matthew in Brisbane and went on to Perth with Bob Carter to persuade Mal Loye, who was wintering in Western Australia, to stay with us.

"Mal drove a very hard bargain. In hindsight, it would have been better if we'd decided to let him go as ultimately he fell out with Bob Carter and that relationship just didn't work out.

"On the field, we showed a deal of promise and improvement and managed to gain promotion to the First Division in the Sunday League."

In 2000, the side won promotion to the first division having been bottom of the table in mid-July.

Coverdale said: "Matthew was keen to play for his country but when I first met him, back in November 1998, he was convinced he didn't have an international future. **211**

KINGAROY, Queensland, Australia
MATTHEW HAYDEN
Born: 29 October 1971
Northamptonshire: 1999 to 2000
Nickname: Haydos
LHB/RM/LB

*Matthew Hayden won a promotion with*
*Northamptonshire in 2000*

212

*David Ripley and David Sales celebrate the 2000 promotion year – and it wasn't just the bubbly going to Salesy's head!*

"On the back of his performances with us over two years he managed to get into the international fold and become one of the world's leading players.

"On the surface you saw a cricketer full of self-confidence but he was always keen to talk to you about his own self-doubts. As I lived close to him I spent quite a lot of time with him.

"I remember one day in particular him spending hours in my lounge at home talking over his insecurities and fears about his cricketing future. One way or another that seemed to help him.

"Matthew led from the front, forged a very good relationship with Bob Carter and won us a promotion.

"Our performances were also boosted by the fact that the bowler Darren Cousins came to the fore and did really well for us."

Hayden's departure at the end of the season elevated David Ripley into the hot seat – for one year only.

Ripley said: "I was vice-captain to Matthew Hayden for two seasons.

"Haydos was brought in as a physically-imposing 'in your face' cricketer who was on a mission to succeed and to get into the Australian team.

"When he left, I skippered the side for one season and the team included Hayden's replacement as overseas player, Mike Hussey.

"Bob Carter had quite a bit to do with bringing Huss in and he was a phenomenal signing for us.

"His nickname of 'Mr Cricket' was so apt, he just seemed to know so much about the game and had a real appetite for it.

"He scored triple centuries against Essex and Gloucestershire and then broke his own county record with an unbeaten 331 off Somerset at Taunton!

"A fantastic batsman, he took over from me as captain after I stepped down and retired at the end of 2001. **214**

*We believe this is a Fields of Maroon and Gold picture exclusive – Matthew Hayden giving freelance photographer Pete Norton the finger following a dismissal at Derby!* **215**

 MOUNT LAWLEY, Western Australia
MICHAEL HUSSEY
Born: 27 May 1975
Northamptonshire: 2001 to 2003
Nickname: Mr Cricket
LHB/RM

*Michael Hussey – an all-action spell*
*with Northamptonshire and three triple*
*centuries in three seasons to boot!*

------------------------------------------------------------------------

"We haven't lost touch. We speak regularly and I took some soundings from Huss before bringing Trent Copeland to the club in 2013, a move which turned out very well for us.

"It speaks volumes that both Haydos and Huss left us and went on to become Aussie legends!"

"In 2001 we were in the top division in both competitions and it was a tough old season.

"On the one-day front, we didn't win a game and painfully struggled on the bowling front.

"We played one game on a featherbed at Cheltenham where we won the toss and yet put them in when we really should have batted. Gloucestershire made 344 off 45 overs and we lost by 83 runs.

"We were without David Sales and Darren Cousins was out with an ankle injury, Paul Taylor was near the end of his career and wasn't that reliable any more.

"In the championship, we fought well at Taunton in the last match of the season but Lancashire did enough to relegate us."

Coverdale added: "It was a difficult season, which saw the side relegated back to the second division after just one season in the top flight. Frankly a number of the players who we recruited let us down.

"The match with Lancashire at the County Ground proved to be the balloon pricker that season as John Crawley and Warren Hegg took Lancashire to victory when they seemed destined to be heading for defeat."

The captaincy baton passed to Mike Hussey in 2002 and, in spite of the new responsibility, he came into his own as a player.

Coverdale said: "He scored three triple centuries for us but, like Hayden before him, could not break through initially into a very strong Australia side.

"He was a lovely guy, there was real gentleness to him and he just loved the game.

"He was a batting machine and I think if he'd become established in the Australian side and toured here in 2005, there is no way we'd have won the Ashes.

"A major distraction in this summer was the massive fall out between Russell Warren and Toby Bailey.       **217**

*July 2001 – Michael Hussey notches the first of his three triple centuries for Northamptonshire, against Essex at Wantage Road*

*And triple century number two – Michael Hussey's number is up at Bristol* **218**

 BLOEMFONTEIN, OFS, South Africa
KEPLER WESSELS
Born: 14 September 1957
Northamptonshire: 2003 to 2006
LHB/RM/OB

"This totally split the dressing room. Bob Carter dug his heels in, believing that Russell should stay and that he would be able to manage the situation.

"Others, including myself, had judged that Russell should leave the club. This was one of the sources of Bob's problems with Mal Loye.

"Bob Carter left the club at the end of the season and his very close friend Duncan Wild left the cricket committee. I was seen by many as the fall guy for Bob's departure."


## MY WAY OR THE HIGHWAY

In 2003, Kepler Wessels was approached to come in as the new head honcho and there was no mistaking the autocratic approach from day one.

The first Championship match against Yorkshire at Headingley in April resulted in total wipeout by an innings and 343 runs, Yorkshire's 673 playing Northamptonshire's 184 and 146.

Wessels was not deterred though and, with Phil Jaques supporting Hussey with some sterling knocks, the side bounced back to achieve a double promotion come September.

Andre Nel, an eccentric firebrand from South Africa, was making friends and influencing people all around the ground.

But Graeme Swann was finding the Kepler Wessels experience hard to handle and Wessels was openly critical about Swann's performances and attitude. **219**

*Peter Willey, who isn't keen on watching cricket, chats to Graham Gooch in the blue seats at the County Ground in 2002 – listening intently is a young David Willey, picking up a few sound tips no doubt!*

Coverdale said: "John Scopes was the chair of the cricket committee and agreed that we should look to bring in Kepler Wessels as head coach.

"It was a final call between Kepler and another South African, Graham Ford. I was hugely impressed by Kepler, everything about him – his knowledge, attitude, approach.

"He'd clearly done his homework on us before he even came to talk to us and had a clear vision as to who he wanted and how he wanted things done. He was a hard, no-nonsense individual but I enjoyed working with him.

"In essence I took on a lot of the man management role and allowed him to get on with the coaching. **220**

GERMISTON, South Africa
ANDRE NEL
Born: 15 June 1977
Northamptonshire: 2003
Alter ego: Gunther
RHB/RFM

*Mike Hussey offers a word of advice or*
*consolation to Andre Nel – or was it to Gunther?!*

------------------------------------------------------------------------

"He was early at the ground every day, even before I was, putting in some archery target practice before the net sessions began.

"It was always 'my way or the highway' with Kepler and there was always going to be a collision course between him and Graeme Swann, who has never been short of self-confidence.                                                **221**

*Two Wantage Road legends – the late great Dennis Brookes and Mike Hussey*

*Northamptonshire's 300 Club – David Sales (1999), Mal Loye (1998), Michael Hussey (2001, 2002 and 2003) and Raman Subba Row (1958) – Australian Chris Rogers (2006) later joined this exclusive club* **222**

"It had been difficult for Graeme. As a young player he was built up very early and then knocked down.

"The South Africa tour under Duncan Fletcher, where he was led astray, was a disaster and at the age of 21 he wasn't going anywhere.

"I was worried because shortly after he joined us I forecast that he would play 30 Test matches for England!

"But I do remember Dennis Brookes telling me not to worry about Graeme's future.

"He said 'don't worry about Graeme, he will be okay by the time he is 26 or 27. He has got to grow up and know his own game'.

"And he was right, but the clash of personality with Kepler Wessels was inevitable and Graeme probably did have to move away from Northampton and freshen things up at a new club.

"The passing of time has proved what we always knew – he was a late developer who has blossomed away from his roots. But he always was, and still remains, a tremendous talent.

"Mike Hussey deferred to Kepler and the year also introduced some other interesting characters.

"As our batting resources looked threadbare we had moved to get in another Aussie-born player Phil Jacques whom no one had heard of.

"He had been recommended by one of our players, Jeff Cook, and to be honest when he arrived he had looked very poor in the nets.

"We got hammered in our first championship game at Yorkshire, by an innings and plenty, I think the club's heaviest defeat.

"Although that match had been an absolute disaster Kepler liked what he saw and told me straightaway that Phil was 'some player'.

"During the year Phil put in some good knocks for us and certainly contributed to a successful season.          **223**

NORTHAMPTON, England
GRAEME SWANN
Born: 24 March 1979
Northamptonshire: 1998 to 2004
RHB/OB

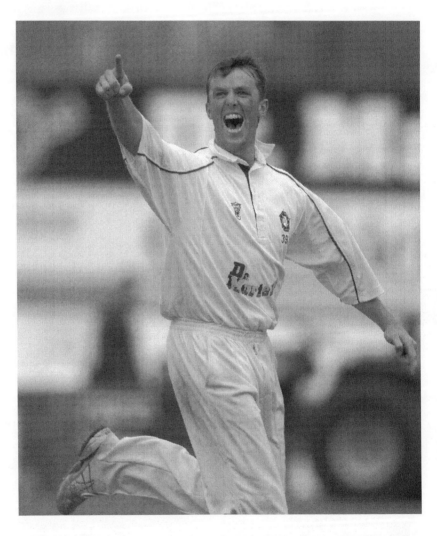

*Graeme Swann – another local lad done good with character, attitude and skill all rolled into one!*          **224**

"And then there was the South African fast bowler Andre Nel, a wonderful guy who really knew how to play to the gallery.

"By the end of the season we'd achieved a double promotion.

"This was my final year with the club, after 19 years, and although there were problems off the field at least on it I was leaving on a high."

Coverdale looks back on his Northamptonshire years with great affection.

He added: "Compared to Yorkshire, where you always felt you were in a goldfish bowl, life at Northamptonshire was very relaxed in comparison.

"With the talent we had at the club from the mid-1980s, certainly between the years of 1987 and 1996, we should have won more than we did.

"We were certainly strong enough, we had some very good players and some great players.

"But perhaps on occasions many were sidetracked by personal ambition and the team suffered as a result.

"Certainly in 1990 I felt we were at our strongest but we fell away alarmingly after a difficult start.

"In the case of Rob Bailey, for example, I personally feel he would have achieved more batting at five rather than three. I think he felt that if he batted at three there was more of a chance of him playing for England and to his credit that is what he did.

"But I think if he stayed at five he would have scored more runs, won us more games, and probably played many more times for his country.

"During my final years at the club, I knew that life for a small county like Northamptonshire was going to change dramatically.

"I was a director of the English Cricket Board by this time so had more of an insight than most into the changes that were taking place. **225**

LUTON, Bedfordshire, England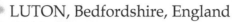
MONTY PANESAR
Born: 25 April 1982
Northamptonshire: 2001 to 2009
Nickname: The Sikh of Tweak
LHB/SLA

*Monty Panesar – the Sikh of Tweak is*
*one of county cricket's most colourful figures*      **226**

"It was becoming tougher each year with the changes to the structure of the county game, the emphasis on Team England and the dispersal of cash among the counties

"We were fortunate to have someone like Lynn Wilson, a generous benefactor with a clear love of the game, for so long.

"Now it is hard for the club financially, especially as the Saints rugby club in recent years have really progressed and taken quite a lot of the cash and corporate support that previously may have gone to the county cricket club."


## THE CULT OF PANESAR

The cult of Monty Panesar ensured that Northamptonshire continued to be seen as a club that played with a smile on its face.

And it was an impression that David Capel was keen to perpetuate when he took over the reins as head coach on the departure of Wessels. For several years his captain was the now mature Sales who summed up their working relationship as coach and skipper.

Sales said: "David and I did work well together, I am very much a realist whereas David was always an optimist. He would perhaps explore other avenues, whereas I'm very black and white. As cricketers we got on very well, we had some key partnerships batting together which was most enjoyable and when I was captain, Capes was very supportive to me and the family as coach.

"We didn't always agree on some aspects, such as team selection, but overall on the whole we reached agreement."

Capel acknowledged the game had now changed markedly from the days when he played. He said: "As a player I would always seek out the umpires in the bar after a day's play and have a good chat with them.

"They were as good as coaches and you could learn an awful lot from them. Players don't do that now."      **227**

*Crossing the sporting divide – Graeme Swann discusses the form with former Northampton Town footballer and manager Ian Sampson*

*Young fans go mad for Monty in a match at the County Ground in 2006*

*'Forget what's happened in the past Mont, it's all bridge under the water now...' – Allan Lamb chats to Monty Panesar*

---

Geoff Cook gave an overview: "Cricket mirrors life in general.

"Gone are the days when you'd go to work and have a few pints from Thursday lunchtime onwards and not do a lot of work on Friday.

"It was a much more social game a few decades ago but, as with most major sports, the professional age has taken over.

"Cricketers are individuals. Some would play better if they'd relaxed a bit the evening before, others would benefit from comparative peace and quiet and an early night.

"These days the exchange of knowledge and sound advice is conveyed by sports science and visual development.

"When I played, we learned through informed discussion and debate from experienced senior professionals and umpires."                    **229**

*Former Northamptonshire players turned umpires Rob Bailey and George Sharp survey the scene at Wantage Road in 2008 – the player/umpire relationship has changed markedly from the days when both were playing*

230

*Where's Monty? – covering up for the absence of Mr Panesar at the team photoshoot!*

------------------------------------------------------------------

## KOLPAK TIME

In his later years at the club helm, David Capel would come to rely heavily on the counsel of another of his captains, Andrew Hall, who followed a long line of South Africans into the corridors of influence at Wantage Road.

He said: "I had read such a lot about Mike Procter and what a great cricketer he was and knew of the high regard that senior players like Clive Rice and Jimmy Cook had for him.

"Kepler Wessels captained both South Africa and Australia and I actually played against him in 1994. He was a hard, disciplined, no-nonsense cricketer and displayed those exact same qualities when he coached.

"Allan Lamb's reputation as a game changer went before him. He could turn things around for his side in a session, sometimes within the space of ten overs. **231**

ST GEORGE, Sydney, Australia
CHRIS ROGERS
Born: 31 August 1977
Northamptonshire: 2006 to 2007
Nickname: Bucky
LHB/LB

"He was a phenomenal competitor, a very positive cricketer and someone who wanted to be as good as he could be.

"I'd had spells at Worcestershire and Kent and returned briefly to South Africa before joining Northamptonshire in 2008.

"Before joining Northamptonshire I really had no experience of David Capel. He was gradually turning round the pitch at Northampton into one which was better suited to seam bowlers.

"Kepler had always favoured encouraging spin and the pitches were never seamer friendly.

"This was one of the things Capes wanted to change. He recognised the need for a far better cricketing surface which encouraged the seam bowler rather than one which quickly took the shine off the ball.

"The fact that the County Ground has now restored that balance in favour of the seamers is pretty much down to the work that Capes put in over the years."

Capel's reign was dominated by a lot of adverse publicity in light of Northamptonshire's fondness for recruiting 'Kolpak' players.

The Kolpak ruling was handed down by the European Court of Justice in May 2003 after Maros Kolpak, a Slovakian handball player, was released from his German club because of a quota on non-European Union players imposed by the German Handball Federation. **232**

JOHANNESBURG, South Africa
ANDREW HALL
Born: 31 July 1975
Northamptonshire: 2008 to present
Nickname: Brosh
RHB/RFM

*Andrew Hall bowling at full tilt for the Steelbacks*

Kolpak claimed this was unfair and the case went all the way to the European Court which ruled in his favour.

The court reiterated the pre-existing Bosman ruling (which had a significant effect on football) and declared that no resident of the European Union should be prevented from working in another part of the EU.

The net effect on cricket, if that had been the end of the saga, would have been minimal because the sport is hardly prevalent on mainland Europe.

But - and this is the important part - at the time of the ruling, Kolpak was not from the EU but from a country with an associate trading relationship.

So the Court of Justice's findings meant that any player from any nation which had such a relationship with the EU could also freely play as a professional.

The main cricket-playing countries with associate trading relationships with the EU included South Africa, Zimbabwe and several in the Caribbean, and the county game saw an influx of cricketers, especially from South Africa, under the Kolpak ruling since 2004.

Northamptonshire, and a number of other counties, recruited heavily from this investment stream and Hall supported the club's policy. He said: "Capes also utilised senior overseas players like Lance Klusener, Nicky Boje, Johan van der Wath and Johann Louw and had to withstand a great deal of criticism because the Kolpak signings were controversial and the England Cricket Board was not happy.

"But it was a very good plan for Northamptonshire at that time. They had a few promising youngsters coming through, but not the number that have come through more recently.

"Capes felt the way forward was for the senior players to help coach and advise them. He wanted each senior player leading in specific areas, developing a game plan and displaying professionalism.                                **234**

DURBAN, Natal, South Africa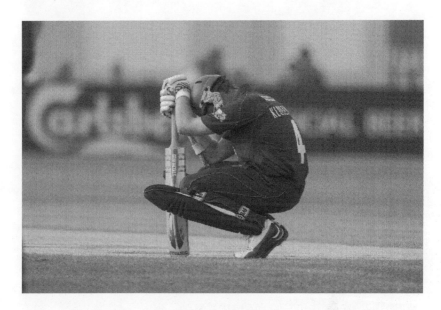
LANCE KLUSENER
Born: 4 September 1971
Northamptonshire: 2004 to 2008
Nickname: Zulu
LHB/RFM

*Lance Klusener – an explosive talent who made his mark at Wantage Road, notably playing for South Africa against Sri Lanka in the 1999 Cricket World Cup some years before joining Northamptonshire*

--------------------------------------------------------------

"It is a tribute to his coaching and management that the club now has young players of the calibre of Ollie Stone, Ben Duckett and David Murphy on its books, while others like Alex Wakely and David Willey have established themselves in the side. **235**

*David Capel – head coach and director of cricket!*

-----------------------------------------------------------------

"Capes was always on the side of the promising young player, you have to remember he was heavily involved in the club's Academy for many years.

"Alex Wakely is a really good talent and if he gets his mind right will go a very long way.

"And there was no doubt at all that David Willey was also a very good cricketer, right from the moment he scored a fifty in his first match against Leicestershire.

"The club has reaped the rewards of Capes' labours and in many ways he did not have the best of fortune in the top job.

"Twice in three seasons he missed promotion to the first division by just one point, so narrow are the margins between what is seen as success or failure.

"As captain of the side, I had a good rapport with him. We didn't agree on everything, you wouldn't expect that. **236**

*No hiding place – David Sales, Lance Klusener and Jason Brown take to the field*

"From a cricketing and tactical viewpoint, he always had a very good eye on what was going on with a game.

"And as an all-rounder, he helped me a lot both as a batsman and a bowler. Ours was a good, straightforward working relationship.

"I saw him as an open, straight up, passionate individual who wanted to see Northamptonshire cricket prosper. I could relate to that, we were both very driven for success."


## THE NEW BRIAN REYNOLDS

David Capel's long association with Northamptonshire ended in 2012 when he was dismissed as head coach on the back of a dismal set of one-day results.

Bailey said: "To be involved with one club for a total of 33 years, as has been the case with Capes, is unbelievable. It was a shame that his association finally came to an end in 2012 but nothing can last forever. It was a good innings.

"I can't think of a greater compliment than to say he has become the new Brian Reynolds, Mr Northamptonshire cricket. Both Capes and I have a great deal of affection for Brian, whom we both owe a great deal.

"Like Brian, Capes is a Northamptonshire man who has devoted his life to cricket in the county."

Nigel Felton was on the club committee that had to make the sad decision to relieve Capel of his duties.

He said: "Capes has been coaching for a very long time and does so to a very high standard.

"His strength in coaching is on a one-to-one basis with young players, he is very good explaining the technical aspects of the game and what is required.

"But I would say that, as with his playing, he could be very intense and very passionate when sometimes the issue needed a little more perspective. He couldn't quite take a step back.

*David Ripley – took over the head coaching duties from his former county-team mate David Capel, who was relieved of his duties in 2012*

-------------------------------------------------------------------------

"He did a very good job as head coach at Northamptonshire and had been given many chances to develop and progress the team.

"It wasn't an easy decision to move Capes and put David Ripley in charge. But the time was right, it was the right decision.

"Nothing Capes has ever said to me or the board didn't make perfect sense.

"We made some astute signings when he was in charge, he could certainly spot a cricketer. All in all, he is a very worthy man."

Head coach successor David Ripley also paid tribute to the contribution Capel has made to the development of Northamptonshire cricket.

Ripley, like Capel, got an opportunity to coach with the club once his playing career had come to an end. **239**

He said: "In my early thirties I began to take my coaching badges and I applied for, and was offered, a coaching role at Bedford School.

"At the same time, Northamptonshire were re-organising the development side of the club. I asked if there was anything available and got a role involved with coaching in schools.

"At the schools level it is very hands on, if you are going on a trip you have to organise the bus, the kit, get forms signed and carry out the risk assessments and the like.

"This level of admin was not Capes' strength but I was quite happy to get stuck into it. But if it came to writing a five or six page report, then Capes would love it!

"His great strength was seeing a fault in a player's technique, or a difficulty, and making some good suggestions as to how this might be remedied.

"His strength was in the technical side of the game, I was stronger on the tactical side and we complemented each other well. Capes took to coaching like he did to playing – he spent hours at the ground, his commitment was relentless and admirable.

"To be 33 years at Northamptonshire – from trainee, player, international cricketer, development officer, head coach – is a tremendous effort. I think only Mike Newell at Nottinghamshire comes anywhere close in terms of staying at one club in a cricketing capacity.

"It must have been hard for Capes when he left the club in 2012 because he must have felt he was leaving behind unfinished business. To get so close to promotion on two occasions, missing out by a point each time, was cruel."

Ripley had to pick up a side short on confidence and belief and set about a systemic plan for improvement in 2013.

Bearing in mind the side's severe shortcomings in limited-overs cricket, little could he have envisaged that the year would be rounded off with the Twenty20 trophy sitting proudly in the dusty old cabinet back at Wantage Road! **240**

*'Don't tell 'em Rips ... ... ....' – head coach David Ripley contemplates life leading his platoon into battle, clearly ignoring the motivational messages from the sidelines. As Surrey found out in the Twenty20 Final, 'they don't like it up 'em!'* **241**

## TWENTY20 VISION

Andrew Hall takes up the story of the period of transformation that turned Northamptonshire from hopeless to peerless.

He said: "There were a number of factors which marked out a great improvement in the team's performance in 2013.

"In the Twenty20 competition, we had two overseas players in the side – Cameron White and Richard Levi - who both performed exceptionally well. We had guys on form at the right time and individual players could turn a game in one over and make a massive difference.

"A clear case in point was David Willey in the final against Surrey coming back to the crease following a rain break and smashing 20-odd runs in one over.

"In previous years, we would get individuals making match-winning contributions at various times, but this happened more consistently during 2013.

"One thing we had discussed in the winter was the need for every member of the side to take individual responsibility for the role they played within the team.

"In Twenty20 matches, we didn't want situations where the side would be say 20-3 five overs in.

"That was a big factor in our approach on finals day. We got put in by Essex in the first semi-final and Levi calmly and cautiously played out the first over.

"The previous year, I'm pretty sure we would have panicked at ball four because we hadn't got the scoreboard moving. The opening bat would probably have got out and straight away you hand your opposition the initiative.

"But Levi played the match on his terms and the same applied later when White didn't go for the big hits until the final few overs.

"Fielding wise we were outstanding and we worked a lot on our bowling during a pre-season break in the West Indies.

"We practised 'death' bowling, slower ball bowling, a lot of that sort of stuff. And we instilled in the players that they had to take ownership once they had the ball in their hand.

"There was no enforcement from up above of what people should do and when they should do it.

"You've got the ball in your hand, you are making the decisions and calling the shots.

"It was a case of back yourself and take responsibility. And with that came tremendous self-belief.

"The bowlers all stepped up to the plate but, for me, Lee Daggett was exceptional.

"And the addition of Mohammad Azharullah, and his ability to send down wicket-taking deliveries, allowed us to attack other sides much more than we had done in previous seasons.

"We only used 14 players during the entire Twenty20 competition in 2013 and that stability certainly served us very well.

"We'd used 18 the year before. Even though I got injured after five games and Levi left during the campaign, we were able to keep that togetherness.

"In the final against Surrey, as soon as we sensed it was going to be our day – or night – we knew we had to go out and make the most of it.

"The fact we lost Kyle Coetzer for the final with a wrist injury didn't seem to make any difference to us.

"David Willey was the natural choice to go up the order, we'd opened with him a few times before.

"We just told him to play his natural game, which is what he did. He was aggressive, single-minded and totally destructive.

"It was a fantastic season all round and winning promotion to the first division was also a tremendous achievement.

"The trick now is for the side to consolidate those achievements and build on them in the years ahead.    **243**

"We have to be competitive, that's the main thing we have to take forward.

"If we don't step up we will end up doing what Derbyshire did in 2013 and dropping straight back down a year after getting up.

"We will have a team plan and individual plans which I hope will give us the best opportunity to do well in division one cricket.

"From a personal point of view, I hope I can stay clear of injury and play a full part in the season.

"And I have to say that I am enjoying the senior player role, rather than that of being captain. As skipper, you ended up managing and taking an interest in everything.

"I found that I didn't switch off after a day's play and for a good three hours I was going over situations, could I have done this or that differently.

"As a senior player, you can relax more – hit a few balls, watch the videos and then leave, maybe thinking about things for an hour or so before doing other things. It's a much nicer balance."

Ripley beamed a wide smile of satisfaction and pride when he recalled the Twenty20 campaign of 2013 especially the sensational cricket displayed by his charges on a murky day and night at Edgbaston on 17 August.

He said: "The players were the main drivers behind the improvement that was achieved in 2013.

"At the end of the previous season, we held an honest meeting and put it out there that we needed to improve in one-day cricket.

"The longer game wasn't so much of an issue, because we'd been there or thereabouts and had been unlucky to very narrowly miss out on promotion on a couple of occasions.

"But we felt there hadn't been enough emphasis on the white ball stuff and chief executive David Smith was keen to stress the commercial gains that follow from being successful in one-day cricket. **244**

"For 2013 we recruited with the one-day game in mind, bringing in Matthew Spriegel and Stephen Crook.

"We wanted them for their one-day expertise, their driver for coming to Northampton was the opportunity to play more four-day cricket.

"As coaches we devised programmes for every player on the staff, working off a general template but tweaked for every individual's needs.

"And they were geared to limited-overs cricket, empowering each player to take responsibility for what they could contribute to the team.

"David Sales worked on his reverse sweep shot, James Middlebrook on the conventional sweep, Stephen Peters on his pull shot.

"We varied our team practice sessions, so that the players enjoyed them more and so that it increased their appetite for the game, and worked a lot on 'death' bowling and slower-ball variations which we hadn't given enough emphasis in the past.

"You could get odds of 30/1 for us to win the Twenty20 and we certainly didn't go into the 2013 season aiming to win the competition.

"We'd had a pretty rough year last time round and purely went in with the aim of winning more games in one-day cricket.

"The senior players led by example and the younger members took their lead from them.

"Stephen Peters missed a lot of cricket but still averaged 50 and James Middlebrook enjoyed a fine end to the campaign.

"Andrew Hall was named Championship player of the year and David Sales contributed 900 runs, including three centuries.

"We'd gone to Barbados before the start of the season and got in a good week's practice leading into the start of the Twenty20 tournament we were involved in out there.    **245**

"In our first match against Nottinghamshire we were absolutely annihilated, which was a big disappointment, and although we had a better game against Hampshire we still lost.

"Our first two one-day games back in England both ended in defeats and so we'd played four one-dayers and not won any of them.

"After all the hard work everyone had put in that was gutting.

"Doubts were beginning to surface and even I had a few doubts about everything working out.

"Trent Copeland and Matthew Spriegel, who hadn't been with us in 2012, felt we were admitting defeat in games at half time.

"We had another productive team meeting and Trent and Matthew felt that we lacked self-belief.

"They helped alter the mindset of the players and we then went on to win our next six games.

"Continuity of selection was very important to me. I wanted to keep as settled a side as possible as I felt a similar side would more readily get into the groove of winning games.

"Cameron White was a big influence on us. He brought a steely, competitive Australian edge and no little skill.

"His pacing of an innings in Twenty20 cricket was outstanding and he delivered a masterclass on finals day, making the right decisions at the right times.

"Mohammad Azharullah's performances were a big plus factor and then there was Richard Levi who we went after because I felt we needed a little more firepower.

"Richard had spent some time with Somerset, who actually weren't that complimentary about him, but we liked having him around – a nice bloke who could hit the ball very hard.

"He hasn't scored the quickest Twenty20 international century for nothing!

"Although we haven't got Cameron or Richard in 2014, I hope their legacy will rub off on the likes of Alex Wakely, sadly out injured, David Willey and Kyle Coetzer.

"David Willey of course is a dynamic cricketer, and anyone who watched us at Edgbaston on finals day will know that.

"He can excel with bat and ball and, like his father Peter, he's a winner. He just needs to find a little more consistency.

"Without Kyle's injury in the final, he wouldn't have opened the batting against Surrey.

"But he showed what he can do from the off with devastating effect and that is certainly an option we will have to consider going forward.

"I don't think there are any natural similarities between the way David plays and the way his father used to play.

"Peter Willey was a favourite of mine when I was a lad and both he and David Steele always made my England XI.

"But both David and Peter have that winning mentality and David is lucky he comes from a very supportive family.

"Peter doesn't come to many games, he's not a great cricket watcher, but he is a great support and mentor to David. However you can't keep David's mum Charmaine away from watching!

"And a big mention too for the way Alex Wakely captained the one-day side in 2013. He did a great job throughout the Twenty20 tournament and showed great tactical awareness for a player still young.

"He had Kyle Coetzer bowling in the semi-final with Essex, which certainly wasn't in our template!

"But the move paid off and he also made a significant contribution with the bat. His performances in four-day cricket have not taken off as yet and that is an area where we are keen to see him improve.

"He is currently averaging 28 in Championship cricket but he is ten runs better than that and so 2014 is a big season for him in that respect. **247**

HAMMERSMITH, London, England
ALEX WAKELY
Born: 3 November 1988
Northamptonshire: 2004 to present
RHB/OB

"Going into finals day we were still the outsiders because the three other teams from the strong southern group all had their backers.

"Hampshire had won the Twenty20 the year before and were the favourites, Essex were fancied because they had beaten a strong Nottinghamshire side in the quarter-final and Surrey were recognised as a strong and solid all-round unit.

"There weren't many giving us the time of day but we kept our nerve when it got tricky in the semi-final against Essex and opened out at the end of a phenomenal run chase, winning by seven wickets with 11 balls to spare.

"And the final against Surrey was just a perfect game. We had lost the toss and were put in and had to contend with a rain interruption.

"But David Willey had the bit between his teeth and that evening was just Boys' Own stuff as far as he was concerned, it was magnificent.

"Credit to him and the rest of the players that night. We just played so well and to win a trophy after 21 years felt so good.

"As a player, I played in six Lord's finals and won just one of them in days when we had money and could field a decent side.

"These days we have to balance our books and cannot afford to bring in players for all seasons and for all competitions.

"I just hope we don't have to wait another 21 years for the next trophy to come along!"

**248**

*The Steelbacks enjoy their triumphant open-top bus ride to Northampton's Guildhall with the Twenty20 Trophy*

------------------------------------------------------------

## FIRST TO LAST!

David Ripley is looking forward to the future but acknowledges it will be a testing one for Northamptonshire, one of the smaller fry among the big fishes vying for territory in the top flight of English cricket.

Consolidation in the first division will represent success for Northamptonshire – that will be tough, so too maintaining momentum in the one-day game with expectation and interest higher than in many a long year.

Ripley pointed out that the side's focus in 2014, unlike the previous year, will be firmly on the longer game and cementing Northamptonshire's position in the top flight.

He added: "I hope we can take the same ethos and spirit forward into our one-day cricket although we will be missing our two overseas big hitters.

"Jackson Bird was due to have come in as our overseas player, to play a bit of Championship and one-day cricket but has been advised to rest a back injury. **249**

NORTHAMPTON, England
DAVID WILLEY
Born: 28 February 1990
Northamptonshire: 2009 to present
LHB/LFM

*First to last...*
*Peter Willey, the man of the match in the 1976 final of the Gillette Cup, Northamptonshire's first major trophy, inspects his son David's bat.*
*Willey senior opened Northamptonshire's innings and hit 65 to defeat Lancashire by four wickets at Lord's.*
*Almost 37 years later Willey junior, opening the Steelbacks innings, clubbed 60 in a 102-run victory over Surrey in the Twenty20 Blast Final at Lord's, Northamptonshire's last major trophy.*
*He too was named man of the match for a display that also included a catch, a run out and four wickets, including a hat-trick!*                **250**

"Our focus will be on the red ball, even during pre-season in Barbados where we want to get the Twenty20 stuff out the way as quickly as possible.

"I have to accept that we will be one of the weaker sides in the division as there is a hierarchy and the likes of champions Durham, Nottinghamshire, Sussex, Warwickshire and Somerset will probably be battling it out for the title again.

Lancashire were promoted as champions with us and the only big player missing from the party is Surrey, who were relegated to division two.

"Every time we've been promoted in the past we've gone straight back down. The trick is to stay in the first division this time.

"I'm very excited at the prospect of playing some very good teams in some big Test arenas.

"It will also be good pitting my coaching and managerial skills against some very familiar faces.

"Mark Robinson has done a tremendous job at Sussex, continuing the good work started by Peter Moores.

"I found myself singing from the same hymn sheet as Robbo when we were both at Northamptonshire, we were both a little quiet and both worried about being accepted by the bigger names in the dressing room.

"He's done it his own way at Hove and, similarly, I hope I can emulate him and get some success for Northamptonshire.

"Only Northamptonshire and Somerset have never won the County Championship.

"I would love to be the person to help set that record straight.

"Former colleagues Wayne Noon and Alan Walker are also doing well in coaching roles at Nottinghamshire and Durham respectively.

"Wayne apart, we are all signed up members of the Yorkshire mafia!"

Felton considered the changing face of county cricket from that which he knew in the days he, Ripley and Capel shared a dressing room at Wantage Road.

He said: "In the 1980s of course, county cricket was still full of Test cricketers, these were the days before central contracts.

"The difference in quality between the county game and Test cricket these days must be huge.

"County cricket was a very different product then and there are many people who look back fondly at those days for many different reasons.

"The England set up was not as good as it is now so I expect the county game's loss had been the international team's gain.

"Psychology did not come into play in the 1980s, before that it would have been interpreted as a sign of weakness.

"Nowadays the players are supported fully on and off the field and undergo rigorous coaching and fitness regimes.

"If you look at the international game now, with Test cricket, international one-day competitions and the Indian Premier League, there is more crossover between the elite cricketers now than ever before.

"The networking opportunities at that level are many and what is now happening at international level is how county cricket used to be.

"One thing that hasn't changed though, either at county or international level, is the dressing room. That will always be the same."

The foundations for Northamptonshire's success in 2013 were laid in the Capel era.

The Kolpak signings introduced by Capel – a policy also pursued by the likes of Leicestershire, Kent, Somerset and Surrey as well as Northamptonshire – paid off.

At Wantage Road the influx of Kolpak players was a development strategy, enabling a financially-strapped club to bring in experienced players to nurture the young talent.   **252**

And it was experience from overseas that ultimately paved the way to Twenty20 glory.

Looking around the County Ground early in 2014, following my final interview with David Ripley, the old place has certainly changed from the good old days of the 1970s.

Modern seated areas now circle the ground, the indoor cricket centre is a beacon where once the football ground stood. Its hinterland is landscaped and has seen a good brush in recent years.

The three-card trick would no longer work and the link to the neighbouring County Tavern pub has been bricked up.

In the summer of 2014, Sir Tom Jones is scheduled to stage quite a different performance with an open-air concert on the ground.

Back in my youth there were concerts on the ground but the likes of Adam and the Ants and Altered Images were confined to the indoor school, which still smells the same now as it did then by the way.

And yes some things don't change – the gatemen still roll off the conveyor belt in their white smocks, there still aren't many people watching Championship cricket and those that do still like to moan.

Which is a little harsh as the commitment to attack and entertain at Wantage Road has spanned the generations.

The ground may not be the prettiest but watching cricket in Northampton has rarely been dull.

So if you are stopping off in town on your way to somewhere else, do pay a visit to Wantage Road and take in some cricket.

The fields are still maroon and gold. That too will always stay the same.

Made in the USA
Charleston, SC
19 April 2014